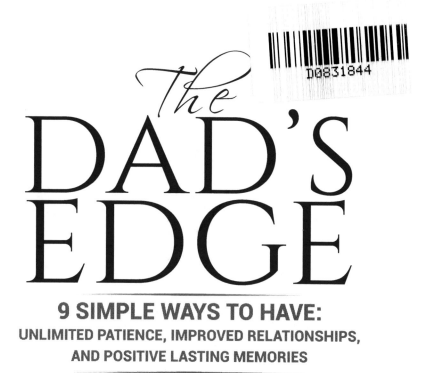

The DAD'S EDGE

9 SIMPLE WAYS TO HAVE:
UNLIMITED PATIENCE, IMPROVED RELATIONSHIPS, AND POSITIVE LASTING MEMORIES

LARRY HAGNER

Copyright ©2015 Larry Hagner
ISBN-13: 978-0692526873
ISBN-10: 0692526870

TABLE of CONTENTS

DEDICATION

To JESSICA

You are truly the love of my life. I have never met a more patient, more loving, or forgiving woman. When we met twenty years ago, I truly felt like a broken young man. I was not good at relationships. I didn't have many life skills. Your love and support has inspired me to be a better man. You have taught me about life, love, and parenting. Words cannot describe how much you mean to me. I love you more than anything and this book would not be possible without your support.

DEDICATION

To MY OLDEST SON, ETHAN

As I complete this book, you are only nine years old. However, you amaze me every single day. You are so affectionate, loving, and considerate. You have so many aspiring life skills at such a young age. You are so genuinely curious about the world around you and you have such a positive outlook on life. You are going to grow up into an amazing young man. I love you, Ethan.

To MY MIDDLE SON, MASON

As I complete this book, you are only seven years old. However, you too never cease to amaze me. Your funny personality always keeps our family laughing. I love how affectionate you are. You are always wanting hugs, kisses, and to sit on my lap. I truly cherish that about you. You will also grow up to be an amazing young man. I love you, Mason.

To MY YOUNGEST SON, LAWSON

As I complete this book, you are only 18 months old. You have been such a joy to our lives. Your funny little personality always makes everyone in the family laugh. I feel so honored to be your Dad and can't wait to see the man you will become. I love you, Lawson.

To MY SON IN HEAVEN, GABRIEL

Unfortunately, you passed away when I began working on this last chapter. You passed away too soon and at such a young age. However, I dedicated the last chapter in this book to you. Losing you was one of the most difficult experiences of my life. However, it has made our family stronger and closer. I know we will meet again when my time is finished here. I love you, Gabriel.

INTRODUCTION

This book is dedicated to the everyday Dad. It's dedicated *to you: The man* who is reading this right now.

It's dedicated to the men *like you* who desire to step up their game as men, husbands, fathers, and significant others.

The "Dad Role" has changed significantly over the past several decades. In my opinion, being a Dad is harder now than it ever has been. However, we are seeing a dramatic shift in the modern approach to being a Dad. Dads today have more desire to step up and improve the connection with their kids than ever before. The stereotypical "Provider Dad" (where a Dad only brings home a paycheck) is a thing of the past. Whether we admit it or not, Dads today want to leave a legacy that involves something far greater than money or material possessions.

Dads today desire a deep connection with their kids, an opportunity to instill character, purpose, and manners; the joy of creating loving and lasting memories with their kids, and most of all, the chance to become a powerful force for good in their child's life.

We Dads want to be more involved.

We want to connect.

Overall, we want to enjoy our journey as fathers. No father wants to live with any regrets. None of us want to be lying on our deathbeds mourning what might have been.

HERE'S THE DILEMMA

Most of us simply struggle with knowing how to do all of these things and do them well. We are so busy putting ourselves down, telling ourselves that we are failing, and trying to measure up to some crazy notion of perfection.

Not only is being a father extremely difficult, but we also have a really hard time enjoying it. For most of us, the journey of fatherhood can be daunting because there really is no "road map."

The Dad's Edge is all about giving you strategies to become that Dad you want to be. It is about giving tips to help you with the small changes that will lead to a big transformation. It's all about giving you that "road map." When we arm ourselves with strategy, purpose, and confidence, there is nothing that can stand in our way.

This book will not necessarily give you any parenting tips for how to discipline your children. In a way, this book is really not even about parenting.

Here's the truth: this book is all about *YOU.*

It's dedicated to help you become the best version of yourself, so you can give your best to your kids. Once we become the best versions of ourselves, being a better Dad is simply a byproduct of the process.

This book is all about giving you critical tools and resources to avoid the most common pitfalls that trip up almost every Dad out there. It's meant to help you quiet your "fear and stress chatter." Your "fear and stress chatter" is the part of your brain and conscience that always seems to yammer away at your self-worth, self-confidence, and self-love. It's that voice that likes to constantly remind you that you aren't good enough. It's the voice that talks you out of taking risks, living life to the fullest, and ultimately talks you out of being the Dad you want to be.

The fact that you have bought this book proves at least one thing: You desire to be a better Dad. It also proves that you want to unlock the secrets to an enjoyable life, not only with your kids, but yourself and everyone around you. So, with that being said, I want to congratulate you for taking the time to "up your Dad Game." Some of the best investments we make in life are the investments in ourselves. The dividends and payoffs come in the form of greater self assurance, confidence, and an improved skill level in anticipating challenges. Mastering these skills will result in improved relationships with our kids and spouses, and just an overall feeling of enjoyment and fulfillment in life.

Sound daunting? To be honest, it is quite a bit easier than you think. This book is a compilation of my own experiences, efforts at self-improvement, healing, and hours upon hours of interacting with Dads just like you.

DISCLAIMERS

Let me start off with some disclaimers. I am not a professional. I have no accolades, certifications, or fancy titles after my name. To be honest, it's not even something I would want. I am truly no different from you. Perhaps the only difference is my journey as a child, as an adolescent, a young adult, a father up until now, and years of self-improvement study.

Life has taught me that every single person has "a story." Behind every face there has been a life filled with struggles, obstacles, and accomplishments. My story and background is not exactly the norm and it has forced me to dive deep into self-improvement. Over the past several years, I have begun to learn:

- How our perception is our reality and we choose our perception

- How, if we want to change our emotions, we must change our state

- How our behavior becomes our habits (whether they are good or bad)

- How our habits become our values

- How we must win in our mind first no matter what challenge we are faced with

- How to quiet the "Fear and Stress Chatter" that always wants to bring us down

- How to feed our positive self-worth, purpose, and passion

- How to live and love with purpose on purpose

- How to have more patience, no matter how chaotic the situation

- How to deepen and strengthen our relationships with our wives

- How to become the best version of ourselves

Before we dive into all that good stuff, let me give you some of my background and why I am so passionate about fatherhood. To be honest, it all stems from not having a father figure in my life growing up. Not only did I not have a stable father in my life, but during the rare times I *did have* a male figure in my life growing up, it was never a positive one. So, I learned firsthand how incredibly devastating it can be growing up without a positive father figure.

My childhood affected my approach to being a Dad. Because of my experiences, I made three resolutions:

First, when it came time for me to be a father, I was going to constantly push myself to grow, learn, and adapt to whatever challenges came my way.

Second, I would always be there for my kids. No matter what the need would be, I would always be present and strive to be a positive role model.

Third, being a father is a PRIVILEGE. It is nothing short of amazing! However, just as anything else in life, we are not born with the skills and knowledge to naturally be the best we can be.

Parenthood is one area of our life that is so wonderful, yet so humbling because it is a constant learning process. If we do not have the right mindset, it can be a very long and tough road. In actuality, it should be enjoyable. Learning the skills and strategies for being the best version of ourselves takes constant work, patience, and a sense of humor.

MY BACKGROUND

To understand where I am coming from, it may help you to know a little bit about my own story. As I write this book, I am just turning thirty-nine years old. I am blessed with an amazing wife, Jessica, and three wonderful boys: Ethan (8), Mason (6), Lawson (9 months), and Gabriel (He's our son in heaven. I will go into this in the last chapter). I have known Jessica for eighteen years. We met when we were both in college. We have been married for eleven years and we have a great relationship. We have a great relationship for one good reason: we work at it constantly. We *choose* to love each other with passion, purpose, and commitment. We have each other's back no matter what. I'm not saying every day is easy. A successful marriage is a two-way street. Some people believe it is "50-50." Well, I'm here to tell you it isn't. If you want your marriage to work and you want to have the strength for the tough times ahead it must be "100-100." Each person gives all they have and that is that.

Our family situation is similar to that of others. I am the bread winner and Jessica stays home with the boys. My job forces me to travel weekly (one to three days a week), so we decided six years ago that we needed an "anchor" at home. It was important to both of us that the boys always had one of us home in their early years. I must say, we have to cut corners financially to make it work, but the returns on that investment pay dividends.

MY CHILDHOOD

I am going to dive a little deeper into my childhood because it truly shaped who I am today, what I stand for, and why I am so motivated to constantly up my "Dad Game" and help other Dads as well.

I was born in California in 1975. My father was (and is) Larry and my mother Deb. They met and got married young in 1971. From what I understand, they most likely jumped into getting married too soon. My mom was twenty-one and my dad twenty-two. The marriage went through its ups and downs, and it was an emotional roller coaster ride for both of them. Four years into the marriage, I was born. By that time, the relationship was beginning to come to an end.

My parents' divorce was extremely bitter. My mom and dad decided to move back to St. Louis, Missouri (where both of their families lived). I obviously don't remember specific details, because I was just a baby. However, I have no recollection of my father being in my life at a young age. In his defense, I believe the situation between him and my mom was so bitter that he wasn't able to see me as much as he wanted to.

Up to the age of four, I had no recollection of my dad being in the picture because quite frankly, he wasn't. I was raised exclusively by my mom. I had no frame of reference for a "Dad." All I knew is that I didn't have one and all my other preschool friends did. But this really didn't bother me. I was just a little guy; so I had no idea how the whole Dad thing worked. I just thought that the Mom eventually found a Dad for the kids and maybe my mom had not found one yet. So, I really didn't feel like I was missing out on much. My mom and I got along great and I was a happy kid.

When I was four, my mom met a man named Joe. I still remember the first day I met him, because the first thing I said to him literally made the room go quiet. I remember him coming over and walking through the front door. He was in a suit, carrying a briefcase, and holding a trench coat. I remember getting the feeling of "wow…this is what it must be like when a Dad comes home from work." To be honest, it was a very odd and exciting feeling. I never had a male parenting figure in my life up until this point.

My mom introduced me to him and without hesitating I boldly asked: "Are you going to be my Daddy?"

Show-stopping comment, right? Looking back on it, you could literally feel the air come right out of the room. I couldn't help myself. I was naturally a pretty curious and bold kid. So, not much has changed in thirty-five years.

I remember Joe's eyes getting very wide. Then he laughed awkwardly. I remember my mom not knowing what to say and perhaps being a bit embarrassed. After all, she had just started dating him and now he probably thought she expected him to be committed! Poor guy! He had no idea what he just walked into! As for me, I was so excited! I thought my mom had found our family a Dad!

Even though it was thirty-five years ago, I still remember that night like it was yesterday. Joe and I got along great. I remember him playing with me and talking to me a lot. I even remember the two of us putting on motorcycle helmets and acting like we were Ponch and John from CHIPS, my favorite show at the time. (For you younger guys, CHIPS was a show back in the 70s that was all about two motorcycle highway patrol cops. It was a great show!)

ENTER MY STEPDAD FROM AGES FIVE TO TEN
Fast forward one year later: My mom and Joe got married. I remember being in the wedding, being at the reception, and being extremely happy that our family was now complete. I finally had a Dad! Life was good. It was such an exciting time.

Joe had a great job with Citicorp and it allowed my mom to quit her job and stay home with me. My mom and I continued to get along great. Joe traveled almost every week, all week long for work. So, I really only got to see him on the weekends. But that didn't bother me. I got to be with my mom during the week and still got to see him on the weekends. Joe and I didn't do a whole lot together. We went to a football game every now and again. He came to my sporting events when he could, but overall, he was pretty busy with work.

TWO BIG SURPRISES
When I was seven years old, two things happened: First, up until this time in my life, I had no idea that there was another man out there who was my biological father. After all, I had no recollection of him. I

hadn't seen him since I was a year old. So, I continued to stay under the impression that Joe was my real father and that was that.

SURPRISE #1

When I was in second grade, I found out that Joe had indeed adopted me and I had another biological father out there that I didn't know. Again, this didn't really bother me. I didn't know life any other way.

SURPRISE #2

The second surprise wasn't so easy to deal with. Joe started to become a very heavy drinker and the marriage started to deteriorate. Not only did the relationship start to fail, but Joe also became a violent person when he drank and when tempers flared. He wouldn't hesitate to push me or my mom around. I remember several times when there was more than just pushing. Depending on how much he drank or how mad he would get, he was known to hit pretty hard. This went on for three more years. Our home life became unpredictable. When I think about those three years, the feelings of fear and uncertainty come to mind immediately. On top of that, this was the beginning of an extremely negative relationship with a father figure in my life. Heavy drinking, yelling, outbursts, slaps to the face, spankings, and being pushed became more of a norm. In Joe's defense, I remember him as being one of the nicest men I have ever known when, and only when, he was not drinking. When he was sober, he was actually a pleasure to be around. It was only when the alcohol was flowing that I witnessed another part of his personality taking over. The only problem was that the longer he was in our lives, the more of the "intoxicated personality" we saw. Over time and towards the end of the marriage, I didn't see much of that wonderful sober man very often. Instead, I saw the drunk, angry, depressed, and sometimes violent side of Joe.

AGE TEN – EXIT THE SECOND FATHER

Fast forward again to a few years later when I was ten years old. My mom's relationship with Joe had come to an end. Not only was he out of the house, but after he left, I would never see him again. The man who was supposed to be my father, mentor, and protector was gone for good. For me, this was devastating. For those of you who grew up without a father, you know firsthand how horrible it is growing up without that fatherly love and guidance. I remember this was the beginning of a very dark time in my life as a young kid. There was a part of me that was devastated that he was gone, but also a part of me that was relieved. I was sad because I no longer had that male role model in my life. But I was relieved because I knew there would be no more late night arguments between him and my mom—the ones that used to terrify me. I knew if he was gone, he would not be around to hit me or push me around. It was definitely a roller coaster ride of emotions for a ten year old, and at such a young age, I didn't know how to process it all.

I went through two tough years without a Dad in my life. My grades took a beating in school. I had a lot of problems socially with my peers. I was one of those kids who "didn't quite fit in." I began to eat terribly and gain weight. I had almost no self-esteem. The attention that I got in school was usually negative attention. I didn't do well with homework or taking tests. I was only in seventh grade. Looking back on it, I simply began to just give up. There was very little structure at home. My mom had to go back to work and she worked long hours. Looking back on it, I don't know exactly how she did it financially. I know she worked very hard to keep us going.

ANOTHER VERY UNEXPECTED SURPRISE AT THE AGE OF TWELVE
When I was twelve something very unexpected happened. I ended up meeting my biological father.

Let me back up and describe how this all came to fruition.

I was twelve years old and was headed up to the local rec center to play basketball with a friend. I remember walking in the front door, going up to the front desk to check in and get a basketball. The attendant behind the desk looked past me outside and said, "Here comes Mrs. Boyd to pay for ice time for hockey this year." I have no idea why my little twelve-year-old mind became so curious, but something inside me clicked. The only thing I really knew about my biological dad was his name and that he lived in St. Louis. Ever my bold and very curious little self, I took it upon myself to walk right up to her and ask some questions.

"What is your name?" I asked.

I remember her looking at me very puzzled. Yet, there was something so warm and compassionate about her eyes.

She replied hesitantly, "Lisa."

I immediately followed that up with: "Are you married to a guy named Larry?"

She warmly but hesitantly replied, "Yes."

I said, "I know this sounds weird, but I think he is my Dad."

She looked puzzled but yet so compassionate. She simply replied, "Are you Larry?"

I smiled and said, "Yes."

I cannot even begin to tell you what level of happiness and confusion that whole conversation brought me.

She looked at me with her warm compassionate eyes and asked, "Would you like to talk to him?"

Without thinking, I immediately said, "Yes, I would."

We walked over to a pay phone that was just around the corner. There were no cell phones back in 1987. She put a quarter in the pay phone and called home.

He picked up. She tactfully explained what had just happened and told my father that his son would like to talk to him.

I still remember to this day that feeling that came over me when I heard his voice on the other end. He sounded so humbled and as nervous as I did. I can't even remember what we talked about, but it didn't last more than a few minutes. All I know is my heart was racing and I didn't really know what to say.

Before we said goodbye, we decided that it would be a good idea to meet face to face soon. Lisa gave me their home number, then I went home and told my mom what happened. She was obviously shocked. However, she supported me wanting to meet him and she allowed it to happen.

THE DAY WE MET

I called my father and we arranged to meet face to face. I remember the day we met like it was yesterday. I remember being extremely nervous. Several thoughts and emotions ran through my mind. My heart was pounding. I was worried we wouldn't know what to say to each other. Do I shake his hand or give him a hug? What will we talk about? I had so many questions. What can I ask? What is ok to ask? Will he like me? Will I like him?

The day finally came. I got dressed in a suit. I wanted to look my best. I was terribly nervous. I didn't really know what to think or what was to come of all this. Nevertheless, the day had come for us to meet. My mom drove me to the place where I would meet him.

I saw him off in the distance as my mom walked me to our meeting location. It is a surreal moment when you see your father within 100 feet of you for the first time. As I walked closer, I could feel the nervousness build even more. I could tell we resembled each other somewhat. We had similar eyes. As I walked closer, I nervously held out my hand to shake his. Looking up at him, I could tell he was nervous as well. But there was also a compassion in his eyes and maybe even a disbelief that this moment had actually happened. He didn't shake my hand; instead he just grabbed me and hugged me. I remember him saying with a great deal of emotion in his voice, "I've missed you."

It was no doubt a surreal moment for both of us. It had been eleven years. We ended up having lunch together and caught up. I cannot even remember what we talked about because the whole day seemed like a blur. However, I remember it being an awkward, yet really positive experience. I don't think either one of us could really believe the day had come when we could actually meet again. But here it was. Here we were.

THE NEXT FEW MONTHS

We continued to talk and spend some time together over the next few months. I spent time with him, his wife, and my half brother who was two at the time. After those few short months, things began to change a bit. It was nothing that was ever said out loud or an earth shattering event. But I remember that our time together seemed to get awkward and strained. I remember getting the feeling that there was something distracting my dad and weighing heavily on his mind. It was almost as if our time together became somewhat difficult for him. I couldn't quite put my finger on what was happening or causing this change, but there's no doubt our relationship began to change. Eventually, we drifted apart, stopped talking, and stopped spending time together. (There was a reason my father exited my life at that time, but out of respect for everyone involved, I will not go into detail. To be candid, to this day, I truly don't understand why our relationship came to an end. I do know that the dynamics were complicated. After all, my father had remarried, and they already had a small two-year-old and another son on the way. So I have no doubt the dynamics might be difficult for just about anyone in this situation.)

At this point in my life, I was only twelve years old and a lot had happened from a "fatherly standpoint." I lost my biological father once when I was a baby. I was then adopted and raised by my stepdad at five, then lost him when I was ten. I reunited with my biological father once again when I was twelve, only to lose him again after a few short months.

It was my all-time low. Looking back on my life now, I realize how devastated I really was, but didn't know why and didn't understand. I never got into criminal behavior. I never got into drugs or drinking. However, I was definitely a lost child. I had zero self-confidence. I had very little direction. I didn't care about school or grades. At one point during my 8th grade year, I simply gave up on school all together. I ended up failing eighth grade, getting "F's" in every single subject. Devastated to watch all of my classmates graduate and move on to high school, I was forced to repeat 8th grade and switch schools. I was also filled with a great deal of emotional anger. I didn't really have athletics to throw myself into, because to be honest, I was not a good athlete. I became more of an emotional eater. During times of stress, I would eat and eat. I was overweight, not very good at school or sports, and I didn't have a lot of friends. It was a difficult time to say the least.

MY SECOND TRY AT EIGHTH GRADE
Through my second try at eighth grade, things began to turn around from an academic standpoint. I began to focus more on school and my grades were much better. My grades actually turned around so much that I was able to get into a college prep Jesuit High School. My mom definitely could not afford the tuition, but luckily I qualified for a work grant. All throughout high school I would work every Saturday on the high school campus doing "grunt work" (sweeping, mopping, cleaning, etc). It was easy work and it paid for my tuition 100%.

THE HIGH SCHOOL YEARS
During my high school years, my mom continued to date different men who would come and go. Some were more friendly than others. Many

were heavy drinkers and not the best influence. I won't go into a great amount of detail out of respect for my mom, but I will say there was nothing stable in her world of dating and relationships. I got very used to seeing men, who could be "potential father figures," come and go. Throughout this period, I not only lacked a good father figure in my life but also came to experience an unstable and sometimes abusive male presence, depending on the man. Several of them were much like my step-dad Joe—nice on the surface level, but once the alcohol was flowing, they would turn into very different people.

Looking back on my life, it was definitely during those childhood years that I learned how critical a positive father figure can be, how devastating it can be if we don't have one, and how much worse it can be if we have an abusive one. For me, I had all three of those scenarios at different stages of my life. I never learned what to do during those times. However, I did experience several hard lessons of what not to do—lessons I would remember when I became a father myself. Overall, I learned firsthand that the bond between a father and child is incredibly important.

It was during those high school years that I found a very positive outlet and escape from some of the chaos at home. I started working out regularly and joined a local gym. At this point, the more time I could spend at school or in the gym meant less time at home. I would spend all day at school and then a great deal of the evening at the gym. By the middle of my junior year, I really hit a healthy stride. I had lost a lot of weight, was eating right, and working out regularly. More importantly, my grades had improved. I made the Dean's List during my Junior and Senior year of high school. For me, this was such an amazing accomplishment. For a kid who had to repeat eighth grade due to failing every subject, achieving the Dean's List at a college prep school felt awesome. It was the beginning of a new chapter and one that I would continue throughout my life.

COLLEGE BOUND

In 1994, I graduated from high school and moved away to begin a college career at Southeast Missouri State University. I had a burning desire to leave the chaos that was a part of my home life.

I had such a passion for health, wellness, and self-improvement that I began pursuing a degree in Health Management with an emphasis on nutrition. I put myself through school, with student loans and working about twenty-five to thirty hours a week as a personal trainer. The time I spent in college was one of the best times in my life for so many reasons. It was the beginning of my journey into relentless self-improvement and growth. I learned self-reliance by paying my own way through school. Last but not least, I met Jessica, the love of my life.

JESSICA, THE LOVE OF MY LIFE

When I was twenty-eight and after seven years of dating, Jessica and I got married. I know what you are thinking: "SEVEN YEARS OF DATING??" I know right? Here's the thing: I didn't know this then, but looking back, I know why it took me so long to ask for Jessica's hand in marriage.

Jessica is one of a kind. Words cannot describe the amount of patience and love this woman has. She is the oldest of three kids and the only girl. Her mom and dad have been married thirty-seven years. Not only have they been married for a long time, but they also continue to choose to love and support each other. Jessica and her brothers grew up in a home with a great deal of love, support, traditions, faith, and functionality.

It took me so long to come around because, to be honest, as much as I loved her, I always thought I would lose her. Whether it was her decision or mine, I was always afraid the relationship would come to an end. All I knew and all I saw growing up were marriages and relationships that ended in divorce. So, my thought process was, "What is the point of getting married? Marriages ultimately end up in divorce, so why bother?"

The other reason it took so long was because I knew that marriage meant kids. One of my deepest fears was becoming a father. And when I mean my deepest fear, I truly mean one of my most dreaded at that time. It was right up there with death and being homeless. I know that sounds extreme, but it was the absolute truth. I didn't realize why this was such a fear for me at the time, but I do now.

I was terrified to be a father because I didn't want to fail at it. After all, I knew firsthand how devastating it can be when you don't have a father, a father who is abusive, or a father who is not engaged. I was terrified because I felt I had no roadmap or blueprint of what it was to be a good Dad and raise a child in the right way. The only thing I knew was what NOT to do. So, to sum it all up: The reason it took me so long to move in the right direction was FEAR—crippling and debilitating FEAR. I was terrified to fail as a husband and even more terrified to fail as a father.

Here is what I know now after looking back on all of this: *FEAR is what we perceive in our minds. It is the story we continue to tell ourselves of why we can't do something so we don't have to attempt it. The fact of the matter is, all I had to do to become a great Dad and husband was to make a decision. I had to DECIDE to be a good Dad and use some strategies to get out of my own way. Stay tuned. I'll have more to say on that in a little while!*

**FEAR is what we perceive in our minds.
It is the story we continue to tell ourselves of why
we can't do something so we don't have to attempt it.**

2 MORE SURPRISES

When I was thirty, two more unforgettable things happened. First, we had our first son, Ethan. Jess and I couldn't have been more excited. To be honest, I think she was excited and I was more terrified. I was definitely excited to become a Dad. However, the voices of "Fear and Stress" were speaking loudly in my mind. I had this constant internal voice that kept dragging me down. While I enjoyed being a Dad for the first time, I couldn't help but be overtaken by the feeling of terror. Would I fail this child? What if I do this "Dad Thing" wrong? Will our marriage survive all the stress and challenges that come with raising this little guy?

Here is a takeaway tip that will make your life infinitely better. I will get into more detail in later chapters. *If you CHOOSE to listen to that VOICE (and we all have it to some degree), that will be your world. Your perception and your internal dialogue is your REALITY. It is only in learning how to keep that VOICE CALM and embrace that fear that we learn how to overcome it.*

Your perception and your internal dialogue is your REALITY. It is only in learning how to keep that VOICE CALM and embrace that fear that we learn how to overcome it.

MEETING MY BIOLOGICAL FATHER AGAIN
Second, once again for the second time in my life, I crossed paths with my biological father whom I had not seen since I was twelve.

I will never forget it. It was a Wednesday morning in 2005. I went to meet a friend for coffee at Starbucks. We were catching up, enjoying some conversation, and sipping on some coffee when suddenly I looked up and noticed a very familiar face standing in line waiting to order. I knew exactly who he was right away. It had been almost twenty years, but I still recognized him instantly. That exact same feeling came over me when I was twelve and saw him for the first time. I felt a great deal of emotion well up in me. It was a mixture of nervousness, confusion, some hurt, some happiness, and a feeling of not knowing what to do next. It was my biological father whom I had not seen since I was twelve.

Do I go up to him? Do I say anything? If I did what would it be? How awkward would it be? Does he even want to talk to me or see me? Would it just be best I sit here with my head turned away and allow him to walk out and avoid any of this madness? All of these thoughts were whirling through my head all at once. In the end, I decided my course of action was to do nothing. To sit there and hope he didn't notice me and just walk out after getting his coffee.

My friend could see the look of surprise on my face and asked me what was wrong. After I told her who had just walked in the door, she was in disbelief.

Her first question was, "What are you going to say to him?" I told her my plan to basically do nothing—simply taking the easy way out. She couldn't believe that I would have no desire to go up and speak to my father, whom I basically had not known my whole life.

She IMMEDIATELY took it upon herself to make a different decision. She decided in an instant that me taking the easy way out was not an option.

She quickly excused herself from the table and walked right over to him. He was sitting comfortably on a couch reading the paper and sipping on his coffee when she boldly decided to take a seat right next to him. As I sat there alone watching their conversation unfold, I could feel my fight or flight response well up in me. Not that I wanted to fight him, but there was a big part of me that wanted to run for the hills.

Several questions raced through my mind as they did when I first met him when I was twelve. Did I really want to talk to him? Did I really want him to come over and talk to me? If he did, what would I say? What would he say? What would I ask? What would be ok to ask? I had so many unanswered questions. As all these thoughts and emotions ran rampantly through my mind, I continued to watch the two of them talk. After a few minutes, she had obviously stated why she came over to him because I saw him look up and around the room in curiosity.

We then made eye contact. He saw me.

I cannot begin to describe the internal emotion riveting through my mind and heart. I saw him stand up, take a deep breath, and walk towards where I was sitting. He had a look that was a mixture of excitement, yet so incredibly humbled at the same time. He walked up to the table with my friend and asked if it would be ok to sit down and talk for a minute. We awkwardly tried to catch up. This was not a typical situation where you bump into an old high school friend you haven't seen in twenty years. This was something much more for both of us and neither one of us really knew how to comprehend it. We talked for a few minutes. He asked what I did for a living, if I was married, and if I had kids. I told him I was in medical device sales, was married to a great woman, and we had just found out we were pregnant with our first. He looked proud and smiled. We decided to end the conversation, but that it might be a good idea to meet up for breakfast so we could catch up and get to know each other.

Believe it or not, this part of the story has a rare happy ending.

I will not sit here and say that the beginning of trying to get to know my father after thirty years was an easy thing to do. There was a great deal of awkwardness. Neither one of us really knew the rules. After all, our situation was so rare and really had no rules or guidelines. For the past nine years, it has been a "figure it out as we go" mentality. I am proud to say that we have gotten through it just fine.

I not only know my biological father now, but I have a wonderful stepmom (Lisa, who I met when I was twelve), and two awesome half-brothers.

I will say this: My father and I do not exactly have a typical "Dad/Son" relationship. Our situation is obviously not typical. So, it is expected that it would not have the same rules or expectations of a traditional relationship. I do not call him "Dad." That term would not be fitting to our relationship. We have more of a friendship/confidant relationship. We spend a great deal of time together and enjoy each other's company. We talk business, politics, sports, and the joys/challenges of raising boys. I do go to him for advice on certain issues in my life on which I think he has a great perspective. Every now and again, he will even come to me for some business-related advice. My boys know him as "Grandpa." It's a great relationship and I truly enjoy it. I wouldn't want it any different. We have had a handful of conversations about the past and what happened. There were obviously several unfortunate things that happened, but we have decided to focus on the good in our relationship and the future.

Just like anything else in life, I can choose to be angry about the past.

I can choose to live mentally and emotionally in the past.

I can choose to be angry about how things turned out between us when I was younger. But what good would that do either one of us? We can choose to see the good in people, our situations, and past. Or we can simply focus on pain and anger. I choose to not live with the pain and anger. Life is much more enjoyable when the focus is positive.

Quite a wild ride for the first thirty-nine years of life, huh? For a long time I chose to live my life with that "victim mentality." I chose to focus on all the ways I was wronged as a kid, on all the challenges, and how it was not all fair. I have done that on and off my whole life. However, over the past several years, I have immersed myself in the study of human psychology, self-improvement, and being the best version of myself. I have spent countless hours on books, seminars, and self-improvement study. I am not saying that I no longer have a tough day, a bad moment, or don't still hear that Voice of Fear and Stress. I am telling you that I have learned how to starve the Voice of Fear and Stress and feed the Voice of Certainty and Positivity. The secret to all this madness is that no one really tells us HOW to do this. It is an absolute set of learned skills that changes your mentality, focus, and perception.

These sets of skills are the premise and the foundation of this book.

In this book, I'm not saying, "THINK POSITIVE and everything will be fine."

In fact, I can't stand that statement. Why? It is missing the "HOW." *The Dad's Edge* is going to give you the "HOWS." After reading this book, you will have rock solid strategies to become the best version of yourself, improve your relationship with your wife and kids, and enjoy life more. Like I said: Becoming a great Dad is simply a byproduct of becoming the best version of you.

Remember: This book is about YOU. This is not about how to improve those around you or how to control your kids. It's about improving you and how to control you.

So, sit back and get ready, because here we go.

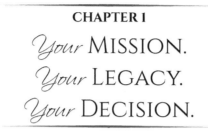

CHAPTER 1

Your MISSION.
Your LEGACY.
Your DECISION.

Do you know what can really make life miserable at times?

The answer might surprise you: It's us. That's right. It's ourselves. It's me. It's you. It is absolutely, positively, ourselves.

Unfortunately, so many of us have negative inner chatter. As men and Dads we have a tendency to put an enormous amount of pressure on ourselves. We can't screw up. Not even once. We need to be exceptional. No, we need to be more than exceptional. We need to be *perfect.*

Every single problem that we have in our lives can literally be drilled down and rooted in our own brain and the stories it tells us. I want you to take a moment and really think about your daily inner chatter. What do you say to yourself quietly? Do you build yourself up or tear yourself down?

Most of us have a voice that can tear us down.

- It's the voice that constantly tells you that you are doing it all wrong

- It tells you that you are not enough. You are not good enough

- It's the voice that second guesses your every move

- It tells you that you are a bad parent

- Or that you are fat

- You are not a lovable person

- You don't deserve something or someone

- You can't

- You never will

- You aren't good at your job

This inner self-talk not only destroys our enjoyment of parenting, but all aspects of life.

OUR WORST FEAR

I will let you in on a secret: There is one ultimate fear we humans share. It is a fear that we all have in common whether you are a father, a mother, a son, a daughter, a grandparent, an employee, or a business owner. It doesn't matter who you are or what you do. We ALL share the same ultimate fear that is so incredibly deeply rooted. If you look at "things" in life that we are afraid of, it literally all boils down to just ONE CORE FEAR.

And here it is:

THE FEAR THAT YOU ARE NOT ENOUGH AND YOU WON'T BE LOVED.

Think about it for a moment: Take anything that you are afraid of or something that is causing you stress. For instance, think about your job for a minute. What really scares you or stresses you out about your job?

You might say:

- "It's the workload…it's hard for me to keep up."

- "I lost a customer or a big client. How will I make up for that?"

- "I am afraid of making a mistake and being let go."

- "I don't get along with all my co-workers and they don't believe I am the right person for my position."

- "My boss is always all over my case."

Then ask yourself why you stress about that in particular? It's because at the root of that perceived stress there is an underlying fear that *"YOU ARE NOT GOOD ENOUGH AT YOUR JOB AND YOU WON'T BE NEEDED and THEREFORE LET GO."*

Think about a troubled relationship. What really scares you and causes you stress about a troubled relationship? Certain things may come to mind such as:

- "We fight about everything."

- "I feel like I am being taken for granted."

- "I feel I am not respected."

- "I don't get the affection that I truly desire."

- "I don't get the recognition and appreciation that I deserve."

All of these perceived stressors can be rooted in one common FEAR: *"Ultimately, I am not enough for this other person, they won't love me, and will leave."*

Are you beginning to see a pattern here?

We see this same thing happen with the relationship with our kids. As our kids get older, they need us less and less. Our relationships with them change. As parents, there is a part of us that so desperately wants to keep that relationship like it was when they were little. They needed us, depended on us, and loved us unconditionally. As parents, we see our kids begin to grow up and pull away from us a bit. This type of situation can cause a tremendous amount of fear and stress. If you really think about the core fear of parenting it's: *"I am or was not enough for my child and now I am going to lose them."*

We underestimate how powerful the mind is. That voice that constantly picks away at you—it's your subconscious. As a result, our subconscious can literally be our worst enemy. It turns our thoughts into our everyday reality. Your mind buys into what it is told over and over.

Simply stopping the madness and turning off that inner chatter will make all the difference in you not only being an amazing dad, but also enjoying the journey of being a dad.

The journey of being a father has peaks and valleys. You don't need mindless negative chatter making your valleys worse and bringing down the enjoyment of your peaks.

OUR FEARS ARE BASED ON THE MEANING WE GIVE THEM
Now that you know what the ultimate fear is in life, "YOU ARE NOT ENOUGH and Therefore YOU WILL NOT BE LOVED," let's dive into something a bit deeper.

Fear is caused by the meaning we give a situation or a stimuli. In other words, two people can experience the exact same situation and stimuli, but perceive it and receive it two different ways.

For example, imagine you are at a professional baseball game. The stadium is sold out and the fans are loud. Your favorite player comes to bat in the final inning and your team is down by one run. The pitcher releases the ball, the batter swings, and the ball heads over the wall! Walk-off homerun! The crowd erupts! You erupt! The cheering is so loud! Everyone around you is happy! The game is a winner! How do you feel? Pretty amazing, right? Your favorite player and home team came through! You experience happiness, exhilaration, and joy.

Here's what happened: your brain gave that situation MEANING. You chose to see all the great things that just happened.

Now, let's take the same situation, but perceived a bit differently. Same thing happens. However, you are a fan for the other team. The homerun was hit and the crowd erupts! Everyone around you is happy and cheering. However, you are pissed! You are not only upset, but the loud noise of the crowd hurts your ears and your ego. The noise of the applause becomes more of an annoyance rather than something joyous. You are unhappy, you feel left out, and you want to leave.

Here's the takeaway: *The situation and the stimuli were the exact same in both scenarios. However, you gave it a very different meaning. Therefore, it affected you much differently. One meaning meant it was the game winner and the other meaning meant it was the game loser. It all depended on the meaning, the focus, and the interpretation. In both scenarios, the stimuli and situation was the same. Ultimately, the meaning is up to us to interpret.*

> In both scenarios, the stimuli and situation was the same.
> Ultimately, the meaning is up to us to interpret.

This is absolutely true in every single area of our lives. **We choose the meaning. That is what we have control over.** We choose the focus. That is what we have control over. We choose the perception, because once again, that is what we have control over.

Here's one more scenario for the everyday Dad: Take two different Dads, but the same situation.

DAD #1

He has a long day at the office. He comes home and walks in the front door. He sees toys scattered from one end of the room to the other. He sees dishes in the sink. He sees the smiles on his kids' faces. He sees that dinner is not on the table. He sees crumbs all over the kitchen floor from a previous meal from earlier in the day. He sees laundry baskets full of clothes sitting outside the laundry room that need to be cleaned.

DAD #1'S REACTION

He's even more stressed than when he walked in the door. Not only did he have a long day, but now he has a long night ahead of him with housework to do. He sees dishes that need to be cleaned, crumbs that need to be swept, and laundry that needs to be washed. Ultimately, he feels more stressed and defeated than two minutes before he walked in the door.

DAD #2

He has a long day at the office. He comes home and walks in the front door. He sees toys scattered from one end of the room to the other. He sees dishes in the sink. He sees the smiles on his kids' faces. He sees that dinner is not on the table. He sees crumbs all over the kitchen floor from a previous meal from earlier in the day. He sees laundry baskets full of clothes sitting outside the laundry room that need to be cleaned.

DAD #2'S REACTION

He is happy to see the smiles on his kids' faces. Everything else is just a blur. He feels happy, fulfilled, and glad to be home after a long day. He welcomes his kids with a big hug and picks them up over his shoulders. Kids are laughing, his wife is smiling, and the room is filled with more joy.

WHAT WAS THE DIFFERENCE?

The difference is Dad #2 CHOOSES to see the good amidst the chaos of his messy home. The meaning he gives the situation is, "I am home, which means I am not at work and I am surrounded by my family who loves me. I see the smiles on my kids' faces, which means they are happy to see me and I am happy to see them. I see we have food on the floor and dishes in the sink, which means I am providing food for my family. I see I have laundry to clean, which means I am able to provide enough clothes for my kids to wear."

Dad #1 chose to give his situation a different meaning. He sees the food on the floor and dishes in the sink, which means more work for him and something else that needs to be done. He sees the laundry, which means he has clothes to clean and another task that will need to be completed. He sees that dinner isn't made and all he can think about is how hungry and exhausted he is.

See the pattern? It is the exact same situation, but the difference in Dad #1 and Dad #2 are:

1. What he chooses to see and focus on.

2. What perception he gives the situation.

3. The meaning he gives the situation.

I can tell you, I spent so much of my time being Dad #1. I had a tendency to always fall into the trap of focusing on the negative. It was an incredibly stressful way to live. There was very little joy and a great deal of stress and burden. It is not the way to live. If you are reading this book, I imagine that is not the way you want to live either. Perhaps you are a wiser man than me and you have already mastered this. Maybe you have already learned that your happiness and focus is your own choice. If so, I applaud you. It took me several years to break myself of that pattern. If you haven't and this situation sounds very familiar, I encourage you to make an immediate change. Look at life and your surroundings in a very different way. Give your situations and circumstances new meaning. Once you have done that life is incredibly more enjoyable. It is not only more enjoyable for you, but for the people who are around you. When you have happiness, joy, and satisfaction, you give it to others. When you choose to have happiness, joy, and satisfaction you bring those qualities out in others. Don't wait to make this critical change. It took me years and I spent way too much of my precious time with that type of mentality.

One final thought: This type of mentality, focus, and perception works in any area of your life. It works in your professional life, family life, and personal life. The above example of coming home to a messy house filled with the smiling kids is just one of several situations we are faced with every minute of every day. We choose to see what we want. We can choose happiness even in the midst of chaos.

The TAKEAWAY TIPS

1. The #1 Human Fear: THE FEAR THAT YOU ARE NOT ENOUGH AND YOU WON'T BE LOVED.

2. Our Fears are based on the meaning we give them.

3. We have the power and the control to choose the meaning in any given situation.

4. Keep in mind the above examples. Do you view your world like Dad #1 (the negative) or like Dad #2 (the positive)? I have lived the majority of my life like Dad #1 and it is not a fun life to live. Choose to look at your situations differently.

CHAPTER 2
Why PERFECTION WILL CRIPPLE YOU AS A DAD

One of the biggest misconceptions about "Dadhood" is we feel we can never make mistakes. We are terrified to make mistakes. We measure our parenting skills up against this perception of "perfection."

This perception of perfect parenting can be crippling to our confidence. When the bar is set that high, we can NEVER achieve the feeling of success as a parent. As a result, we do not enjoy the journey of parenting as much as we should.

When we first become fathers, we feel that we have to and MUST know all the answers. It's part of our "male/primal wiring" to be problem solvers. We view ourselves as "The Rock, The Strength, and the Foundation of our Family." We feel incredibly humbled when we do not have all the answers.

I was truly no different. I still struggle with this every single day. Every day is filled with happiness and challenges. For the longest time, I looked at life as a glass that was half empty. If I had two bad things that happened in one day and ten good things, I would automatically focus on what went wrong that day. That type of mentality can wreak havoc on anyone's level of patience and overall enjoyment of parenting.

One of the best analogies I have ever heard that really drives this point home was from a friend of mine who loves golf more than life itself. He is a highly competitive person and enjoys every minute of time he can spend playing golf. The one thing I always noticed about him when we would play was that no matter how competitive he was, he really never got frustrated when he made a mistake on the golf course. If he severely sliced, missed a putt, or just had a really bad game, he would simply laugh at himself.

One day, when we were out on the course, I asked him what his secret was to not getting frustrated while playing the game that frustrates so many of us. After all, golf has a reputation for bringing out the frustrations in even the calmest player.

He said, "If I always measured myself against Tiger Woods, I would lose the love, passion, and enjoyment of the game."

Hearing that statement was so empowering, and it reminds me of what we men put ourselves through from time to time as Dads. We can be so incredibly hard on ourselves when we set the bar at the "perfection mark." We have a perception that being a Dad means no mistakes. We have a perception that being a Dad means no bad days or bad moments.

Nothing could be further from the truth.

The truth is, there really is no clear roadmap for how to be a successful father. Moreover, being a successful father is not a "one-size fits all" strategy. What works for one Dad may not work for another.

Here is the real key and takeaway: *Have a sense of humor about being a Dad. Have fun with it. You will not only make mistakes, but you will most likely make mistakes on a daily basis. And guess what? That is OK! If you are not making mistakes, then it most likely means you are either checked out or not engaged. In all honesty, if you are reading this book, that is NOT YOU anyway.*

Have a sense of humor about being a Dad.
Have fun with it.
You will not only make mistakes,
but you will most likely make mistakes on a daily basis.

If you make a mistake, apologize for it. If you make a mistake, own it. The best lessons our kids learn from us are what they learn by example. If they witness us being calm, cool, and collected in the midst of chaos that will teach them to handle their stress levels better as they develop. Not only will it be good for your kids to see their dad as that calm, cool, collected person, it is also good for you. It's all about your mentality and focus. If you focus on being perfect and taking any and all mistakes extremely seriously, then hold on tight because the life of fatherhood will be a very bumpy and rough ride. However, if you are ready to get your hands dirty, get engaged, have a sense of humor, and be ready to make mistakes, then let's move forward!

The TAKEAWAY TIPS

1. As a Dad, be prepared to make mistakes and laugh at yourself. If you want to really put a damper on your enjoyment during the journey of fatherhood, make sure you are super hard on yourself and beat yourself up when you make a mistake.

2. When you make a mistake, be the first to openly apologize to your kids and/or wife. Being open about being human and apologizing will teach your kids the same valuable lesson. You are teaching them to be human and mistakes are not necessarily "life-ending," but instead a learning experience from which we all can grow.

3. Know that when you are making mistakes, it means you are more engaged and involved. The player that never makes a mistake is the one that is sitting on the bench. If you are an active, involved, and engaged Dad, you will make mistakes. But that simply shows you are there and present.

4. Remember: You are a Dad, but you are also human. You are most likely doing a better job than you think.

CHAPTER 3
DRASTICALLY IMPROVE
The CONNECTION WITH OUR KIDS
WITH DAILY & WEEKLY TRADITIONS

Unfortunately, I travel for work on a weekly basis. I am not gone too often (one to two days per week), but it is enough that my boys certainly notice. To be totally honest, it is the one area of my job that I cannot stand. Every week, I have to pack my bag and head to some part of the Midwest. While I enjoy my job and providing for my family, the travel wears on me something awful. If you are a traveling Dad or parent, you totally know what I am talking about.

When I have to leave, my boys don't have an easy time with it. And to be honest, neither do I. Traveling and leaving my family is a tough cross to bear.

THE DAILY CONNECTION
Being a Dad gives us the opportunity to connect with our kids on a daily basis. However, how often do we truly seize that opportunity? Our days can start with chaos and end with craziness. On some days we feel like we have been in battle trying to solve the problems of the world. It can become difficult to remember to set aside time each day to talk and connect with each kid. Our lives as Dads can move so fast and furious

that we forget to take a "daily time out." Again, the question is: "How do we take that time out?"

Over the past few years, I have taught Dad workshops. I have had the privilege to work with and learn from thousands of Dads. I have gained the perspective of what successful Dads do on a daily basis to ensure they are giving the relationship with their kids the proper emotional feeding.

One suggestion in particular is to make sure you spend at least five to ten minutes each day with each child. It must be one-on-one and without any distractions. For example, I have found that the best time for me to do this is at night right before bed. I usually put each kid to bed and try and spend at least five minutes with each. The reason that time of day works best for me is because I know I will have guaranteed one-on-one time with each of my boys. That time is sacred. It's our time. There is no TV, no cell phones, no electronics, and no distractions.

Another suggestion is to be prepared with some opened-ended questions to get your kids talking. The reason I suggestion opened-ended questions is because the conversation will be more impactful and it will get them talking. At times, it's not easy for me to carry on a conversation with a seven and nine year old unless I am prepared. If I ask questions like:

"What was the best part of your day? Why?"

"What are three things that you are grateful for today?"

"What were three things that were really tough for you today?"

"What do you like most about school?"

"If you had to do your day over again, what would you do different?"

I know this sounds like pretty simple stuff. However, some of these things don't come to mind unless we are consciously thinking about them and we are present in the moment. Trust me, asking your kids open-ended questions (questions they can't give one word answers to) will add a great deal of connection and humor to your conversation. Even if your child is at an age when they are beginning to pull away and they don't want to talk openly, they will truly appreciate your efforts and may eventually open up. Keep trying and don't give up. Daily connection is super impactful for both you and your kids. Have fun with it. Your kids will always remember it and so will you.

THE WEEKLY ADVENTURE

Now that we have covered a daily connection, let's dive a bit deeper with a weekly connection that is unforgettable for both you and your kids.

For the past several years, I have tried to schedule time with both of my older boys on Saturdays or Sundays. It doesn't always happen due to a sporting event conflict, a family get together, or something else. However, I definitely try to make it a point to do something weekly with the boys (just the three of us). Reason being, I want them to have positive and lasting memories of us having experiences and adventures together.

Every week, we usually set out for a park, a hike, some indoor rock climbing, or even doing some obstacles at a local Ninja Warrior Training facility we have here in town. If the weather is a challenge or we are all a bit tired from a long week of school, work, and sports activities, then sometimes a movie is a much needed activity.

Here's the main point: "The Saturday or Sunday Activity/Adventure" is something my boys and I know is a set day and time when we will all be doing something together. So, even during the week when life and activities get hectic, we all know we have that Saturday/Sunday afternoon to be together and reconnect on a whole different level.

Trust me, it is therapeutic for everyone involved. I love it because it is SET and SACRED time for just my kids and me. My wife loves it, because it gives her a bit of a break. She loves our kids more than life itself, but it also helps her to just reset a little bit. My boys love it, because it is something we all share and experience together.

The TAKEAWAY TIPS

DAILY CONNECTION

1. Choose a time of day that you can devote five to ten minutes of time with each child.

2. The time is one-on-one and sacred with no distractions.

3. Ask "open-ended" questions to get your kid talking and really involved.

4. Have fun with this.

WEEKLY ADVENTURES/CONNECTION

1. Choose a Saturday or Sunday every week to carve out two to four hours of time with just you and your kids.

2. If you work weekends or if you are challenged on time to spend the time on weekends, pick one night during the week.

3. Put it on your calendar. The most difficult part of getting started with this is scheduling the day and the activity. So, at the beginning of every month, schedule the days, times, and what activity you will be doing.

CHAPTER 4

How TO MAKE UNFORGETTABLE MEMORIES EVERY YEAR

In the last chapter, we hit upon the importance of us getting out and spending daily and weekly time with the kids. Now, let's take it one giant step further.

If you are a Dad with more than one child, it can be a challenge to spend one-on-one time with each kiddo. However, it is absolutely essential and critical you take some time out just to spend time with each one.

We can all agree that the dynamics of having all the kids (if you have two or more) can be very different from just having one-on-one time. When we have one-on-one time with one of our kids, they are usually very different compared to when they are with their sibling or siblings. They will usually open up to you more and they feel more important because they know they are getting 100% of your attention.

Since I am a Dad who travels for work, I am physically not present about 20% of the time. When you add that up over a one year period I am gone for 73 days out of 365 days per year. Overall, that adds up to over two months per year that I am not physically present with my kids. It kills me.

A couple of years ago, when Ethan was six and Mason was four, I felt like my work travels were having a big negative impact on both of them. I noticed they were getting to the age that they really started to understand what it meant when I was not going to be home for a day or two. When I would get my suitcase out to pack for my work trip, my boys were usually not happy. At times the complaints were even followed by tears. The boys would tell me that they didn't understand why I always had to leave. As a Dad, this pained me. I think every Dad out there can agree that there is such a fine line between trying to be the substantial provider and a Dad with Purpose.

THE YEARLY ONE-ON-ONE ADVENTURE BEGAN

Because of this challenge, I decided to start a new tradition/adventure with the boys. I decided that I would take each of my boys on a one-on-one yearly trip. After all, I had enough hotel and airline miles to last me a lifetime. Why not put them to some good use?

I decided that I would take each of them to Chicago for our first adventure. Chicago is an amazing adventure with kids if you know how to get around and if you go at the right time of year. It was amazing, to say the least. We checked out the Shedd Aquarium, the Adler Planetarium, the Museum of Science and Industry, and the Willis Tower. Not only was it amazing for them, but it was also amazing for me. It was not only their first time for all these activities, but mine too. So, we got to experience them as an adventure for the first time together. This past year, I took each of them to Colorado Springs, Colorado. We hiked at Pikes Peak Park and Garden of the Gods. We drove to the top of Pikes Peak. We took an ATV tour through the mountains. In fact, the photo on the cover of this book is of Mason and I nearly 10,000 feet up on the summit of a mountain during our trip. It is one of my most cherished photos. It was absolutely amazing and one of the best trips I have ever been on.

The reason I go all out on these trips is because growing up, we never really traveled as a family. So, being able to go to these places now is extremely special because it is usually my first time seeing these places as well. We truly get to experience them together for the first time.

Not only is the experience of exploring and seeing these places for the first time amazing, but more importantly, it is the one-on-one time we get to spend with each other that is the best. There is something about getting away from the everyday grind and exploring uncharted ground together. I cannot even really express it in words, but there is something so liberating about being away from any and all distractions and obligations. When my son and I are on a one-on-one trip, there is no homework, there are no deadlines, no emails, no phone calls, no sporting events we have to be at, and nothing keeping us from focusing on the adventure at hand. While being on these trips I get to know my boys on a whole different level. They open up. We talk about things that we normally would not if we were in our "everyday grind." Best of all, we take pictures and a lot of them. We've made some epic memories that will last a lifetime. My hope is that my boys continue this tradition with their kids because they feed the relationship in such a profound, positive way.

Now, let's talk about how we can incorporate this into your life and the life of your kids. I challenge you to take a one-on-one trip with each of your kids every year. This is an absolute must. Here's the truth: *The trip does NOT have to be extravagant from a cost perspective. Kids don't measure love in DOLLARS. They measure it in TIME. With that being said, you can plan anything from a simple camping trip weekend getaway to a 90-day trip around the world and anything in between. The trip is not about the destination or the activity. It is about the time together and the connection that is created.*

The trip is not about the destination or the activity. It is about the time together and the connection that is created.

I will let you in on a little secret: The most difficult thing about doing this trip is simply scheduling it. Just do it.

The TAKEAWAY TIPS

1. The most difficult part of this whole process is scheduling it. So, do that first!

2. When looking at your calendar you may see other obligations (sporting events, a recital, family reunion, etc). There will always be something else you could be doing. Just schedule it—even if it means you have to sacrifice something else. Ten years from now you won't remember the little league game you missed, but you will remember the trip and adventure you both experienced.

3. The rules are as follows: It has to be for at least forty-eight hours. No texting, no emails, no homework, no obligations. These forty-eight hours are sacred. Nothing distracts you from each other. That's the whole point of going somewhere.

4. Take a camera. A camera is essential. When you get back, sit down with your child and pick your favorite photos. Put them in a collage and hang it on the wall. The best memories are the photos we hang on the wall. They serve as a constant reminder of our most cherished moments.

CHAPTER 5
Discover
UNLIMITED PATIENCE

Patience is the secret sauce of parenting.

Have you ever heard being a parent is the toughest job in the world? I imagine you are shaking your head "yes."

Have you ever heard being a parent is the most rewarding job in the world? Yes again?

The reason you silently shook your head "yes" to both statements is because both are absolutely true.

WHAT IS PATIENCE?
When you think of the word "patience" what comes to mind?

The definition of patience is *"the capacity to accept or tolerate delay, trouble, or suffering without getting angry or upset."*

For some of us, patience is a limited resource. In other words, we think and feel we only have "so much" of it. For others, it seems like they can stand toe-to-toe with life's best punches and never get phased. They can keep on taking shot after shot and keep getting up.

Have you ever wondered what the secret is?

I think I was six years old the first time I saw the movie "Rocky." Everyone knows the story of the Italian Stallion, Rocky Balboa. Rocky was a boxer who was a nobody from Philly. He was given a shot at the title from the world heavyweight champion, Apollo Creed. During the fight, Rocky literally stands toe-to-toe with the champ and takes his best punches. He gets knocked down several times, but constantly gets up and just keeps coming at the champ. At one point in the fight, Rocky had taken so many shots to the face that his eye swelled shut. Instead of throwing in the towel and quitting, he demanded his trainer cut open his eyelid so he could press on. He continued to press on and do the impossible. Even though he lost the fight, he was the only one who went the distance with Apollo Creed. It was that "never giving up" mentality that made all the difference in his next fight with Apollo.

For most of us, life can sometimes feel like we are standing toe-to-toe with the heavyweight champion of the world, taking shot after shot. We find it difficult to keep moving forward when life is throwing her best punches. It's times like these that we feel we have that limited supply of patience.

What happens when we lose our patience?

We are irritable. We are moody. We aren't pleasant to be around. Others probably don't enjoy our company as much.

Losing our patience isn't only about how it affects those around us. It's also about how it affects us internally. It can be a vicious cycle of something, someone, or a situation that irritates us externally, but also what happens to us internally. Not only are we irritated by our external factors, but we also internally beat ourselves up. We start asking ourselves defeating and demoralizing questions like:

"Why can't I handle this?"

"Shouldn't I be able to take on more and tolerate more?"

"Why do I feel I am not up to the task?"

"Am I not good enough?"

When we question ourselves like this, we only make the situation worse.

The purpose of this book is to give you some solid strategies to avoid burnout. It is intended to help you increase your patience with yourself and others. When our patience wears thin, it usually means we are trying to do too much without taking time for our own rest and balance.

Parenting is the most rewarding and fulfilling thing we can do with our lives. We give life to another human being. We protect, love, and guide our children with more love and care than anything else in the whole world. Nothing is more important to us than our kids. We work hard to provide for our families. We sacrifice things we want for the needs of our kids. We love unconditionally and without question. We love nothing more than to see our kids happy and fulfilled.

The reason is:

It makes us happy.
It makes us happy to give and show love.

On the other hand, parenting can humble us like nothing else. At times, parenting can feel like the area of our life where we have the least amount of control or satisfaction. We feel stressed, overwhelmed, overworked, and burnt out. At times we don't feel confident in our parenting skills. It's at these times our patience wears extremely thin.

If we think about the average day of a parent, our days are usually filled with problems to solve. They can start early in the morning when our kids won't get ready for school or start arguing at the breakfast table. The day can also start with an email from a disgruntled boss or customer. Other days, it can start with a disagreement with our spouse. It doesn't really matter how problems or issues show up, because the fact is they always do and they always will.

Challenges and problems are a part of life. Sometimes they will come sporadically. On the other hand, they can come at us non-stop. Problems can sometimes come at us like a tsunami: Wave after wave, day after day. Times like these it feels like life has a hammer and it just keeps chipping away at our patience.

Our patience is controlled by one thing: Ourselves! As much as we like to think our patience is controlled by an outside factor, it actually is not. Patience is a direct result of our chosen response to an external stimulus.

TIP #1
GIVE YOUR CHALLENGING SITUATIONS NEW MEANING
Think of the example in the last chapter about "Dad #1 and Dad #2" coming home from work to a house of smiles and chaos. The most immediate and effective way to have more patience at any moment, at any time is to simply give your situations and circumstances different meanings. If you concentrate on how messy the house is, you will most likely lose that valuable resource (patience) that we all want more of. If you focus your perception and energy towards the smiles on your kids' faces, the dirty laundry means you have clothes to keep you warm, the dishes mean you have food to eat, you will have a very different response and as a result: MORE PATIENCE.

TIP #2
FILL YOUR OWN BUCKET EVERYDAY

As parents, we are always filling the emotional and physical needs of our kids and spouses. Our kids require a great deal of "emotional feeding." We are constantly providing reassurance, encouragement, guidance, discipline, and physical affection.

As a spouse, we are required to wear many unselfish hats as well. We have to be supportive, caring, loving, and generous. We have to be an ear to listen when the other needs to vent or express something. We have to be completely emotionally, spiritually, and physically invested in the relationship to make it work.

Let's face it: Marriage is not a walk in the park. Even the best marriages have issues and complexities. Filling the needs of a spouse can also take a great deal of effort and emotion.

As adults in the workforce, we are always filling the buckets of deadlines, expectations, and requirements. In the workforce, we are problem-solvers. We are usually stretched extremely thin trying to fulfill the everyday demands of our employers. Sometimes we are required to work long hours (sixty plus hours per week) to make ends meet. Some of us even work two jobs.

The theme of being a parent and an adult is constantly being available to someone else's needs and demands.

And that is okay. That's life.

The takeaway here is to recognize how much time, effort, and energy we are putting into everything and everyone around us, while taking very little (if any) time for ourselves.

In order to be our best, we have to take time to take care of ourselves. That may sound selfish or counterproductive, right?

It's not.

Taking time to fill your own bucket, to ensure you are at your best for those around you, is the most unselfish thing you can do. Don't get me wrong: There is a delicate balance between being too selfish and not making hardly any time for your family. For example, we probably all know one person who is a parent and spouse who works so much that they don't see their family. Their work/life balance is completely out of balance. Or we probably know people who are so into a hobby or a sport that they do not have any time to spend with their loved ones.

30-60 Minutes Per Day Just For You
The balance I am talking about is something Tony Robbins calls "Your Daily Hour of Power."

In other words, finding just sixty minutes (no less than thirty minutes) per day in our busy schedules to do something just for us. It is sixty minutes when we do not have to answer a phone or respond to an email. It is a sacred time just for us. It can be writing music, exercise, practicing your golf swing, listening to your favorite inspirational podcast, prayer, meditation, a hobby, or learning a new skill.

It can be whatever "fills your bucket." It can be whatever you want it to be, but you have to give yourself the time and permission to do it.

It has to be positive and uplifting. It has to be something that you feel fulfilled after doing it. For example, think of the last time you did sixty minutes of exercise. After the completion, didn't you feel refreshed, revived, and ready to take on the next challenge? It's because you took just that one hour for yourself. It's because you took that sixty minutes to not answer to anyone but yourself. It's because doing something positive for your mind, body, and spirit is uplifting.

Once you have made that one little tweak to give yourself just one hour per day to disconnect from the daily grind, you will see significant improvement in your overall well-being, your mental clarity, and your patience.

As you read along through the rest of this book, I will give you several more suggestions that will make vast improvements in your everyday life. As you read through each chapter/challenge, I think you will find that most of us have several challenges and inner struggles that we battle every day. It's those inner battles and struggles that can wear down our patience. Once we have a better road map of what to do when these challenges show up, the more equipped we will feel to take them on.

So, let's bring this all full circle.

In order to have more patience at any moment, at any time, you have to give your circumstances and situations new meanings. When confronted with a chaotic situation, change your focus, perceptions, and meanings.

The long-term solution for more patience is to participate in an activity, a recreation, or organization that fills your bucket. By filling your bucket with something positive (exercise, a prayer group, playing an instrument, going to church, playing a quick round of golf, yoga, or volunteering) you are taking time for yourself to do something fulfilling. Remember, doing something fulfilling for yourself is not selfish. In fact, it could be one of most unselfish things you can do for those around you. The more fulfilled and less burnt out you are, the more patience you will have.

The TAKEAWAY TIPS

1. Choose to look at the positives within challenging situations. If you look hard enough, they are right there in front of you.

2. Do something every single day just for yourself for no less than thirty minutes per day.

    Examples:

    - Meditation

    - Prayer

    - Exercise

    - Reading something inspiring

    - Listening to an uplifting audiobook or podcast

CHAPTER 6

EXERCISE:
An HOUR OF POWER

In the last chapter, we talked about ways and activities you can do to fill your bucket and increase your level of patience. If I can offer you one suggestion for your hour of power, it would be to find something you can do to improve your overall health.

The healthier you are, the happier you will be. The healthier you are, the more vibrancy and energy you will have and the happier you will be. The healthier you are, the more active you can be with your kids and the happier you will be. The healthier you are, the more attractive you will be to your spouse and the happier you will be. See the pattern here?

Health and exercise play a huge role in being the best version of yourself. The way you feel physically has a direct impact on how you feel emotionally. The better you feel physically, the better you will feel emotionally. Now that we have taken a deep dive into some solid strategies to change your focus, mentality, and perception (your "inside"), let's take a look at the advantages to doing something for your body—your "outside."

Before we dive into the benefits of exercise, you need to know something right here and now. Exercise doesn't have to be something that you don't enjoy. Physical activity doesn't demand a "one size fits all" approach. Some people enjoy weight training and bodybuilding. Others enjoy Crossfit, "tough mudder" races, and marathons. Others really like yoga, cycling, or playing basketball. Some guys cringe at the very thought of setting foot in a gym. And guess what? That's ok. The gym is not for everyone. The main take away here is that you carve out thirty to sixty minutes every day (or at least three times a week) to do something for your health. It has to be something you look forward to and really enjoy. It has to be something that really excites you and you won't dread doing it. That's the secret to sticking to any exercise plan long term: You have to enjoy it.

Let me say that again: The secret to sticking to any exercise plan long term is that you have to enjoy it.

I am an avid "gym rat." I have been going to the gym religiously at least three days per week for the past twenty years. I go to the gym because I truly enjoy it. To be honest, I am terrible at golf, I can't shoot a basketball, and I don't enjoy running long distances. Let's just say outside the gym, I am not the most athletic person. I was not a good athlete growing up and I most likely will never be a great athlete. The gym is what I enjoy. I have been able to sustain twenty years of consistent exercise because I enjoy going to the gym.

I go to the gym for several reasons:

1. It's good for my physical health. The older I get the more I see the importance of taking care of my body. The body is just like anything else in life: If you don't use it, you lose it. Nothing can impact your quality of life like your health. It's difficult to enjoy the little things in life when you have a health ailment. Ask any person who has chronic back pain how life was before and after the onset of their pain.

2. It's good for my mental health. If I go several days without my sixty minutes in the gym, I start to become irritable. It's difficult for me to handle the everyday curveballs of life when I do not take an opportunity to relieve stress. The more consistent I am in the gym, the more capable I am to handle the challenges of work and family.

3. It gives me an hour to not answer to anyone. Taking that sixty minutes per day is more than just exercise. It's an opportunity to not answer to anyone. It's an opportunity to get my own thoughts and frame of mind centered. There is great relief in knowing I don't have to answer an email, a phone call (unless it's an emergency of course), or settle sibling rivalry between my kids.

4. I feel more confident when I exercise. Confidence plays a critical role in our business and personal lives. Feeling more confident makes me a better father, husband, and employee. The better I feel about myself, the better I will be for those who are around me.

5. It helps me retain my youth. The more youthful and vibrant I feel, the better I will be able to play and be active with my kids. The body was built for movement. It was not designed to stand still and be sedentary.

6. Exercise improves sex life. Exercise plays so many critical roles in the health of our sex lives. Exercise increases testosterone levels, which in turn increases sex drive. Exercise builds your body to look and feel more attractive to your spouse. As a result, the better our sex lives, the more fulfilled we feel. Sex is a critical part of any healthy relationship. Going too long without it can make us irritable, disconnected, and more stressed. So, make sure you understand this important connection. Exercise improves sex life and improved sex life improves quality of life.

7. It's a great example to set for my kids. My kids know that I go to the gym almost every day. It is part of my lifestyle and routine. It is just as routine for me to go to the gym every day as it is for them to brush their teeth. It gives me a great opportunity to teach them the benefits of a healthy lifestyle. My boys and I play sports, we run, we do sit-ups and pushups, and we do it with a mentality that we are taking care of our bodies and minds. The older they get, the more this will become a part of them as well.

There are several additional reasons I go to the gym for my hour of power. The question I have for you is what do you do or what would you do for sixty minutes every day? You cannot use the excuse that you do not have time. We all have the same hours in a day. We all have 86,400 seconds every single day to make choices. If you don't have something that you do to daily to recharge yourself, make it a point find something that will.

CHAPTER 7
THREE SIMPLE & FUNDAMENTAL WAYS *To* CONNECT WITH YOUR WIFE NO MATTER HOW BUSY YOU ARE

Jessica and I have been married for eleven years. I have known her for eighteen years. We met in college when she was a freshman and I was a sophomore. We had an instant connection. We dated for seven years before getting married. Knowing her for so long, I can tell you there have been peaks and valleys in our relationship. There have been times when we are extremely close and everything seems to be amazing. There have been other times when it is a struggle to find time to connect with each other.

As I write this book right now, this very minute, I can tell you we have been going through a time when it has been more difficult to connect than usual. In the past year, we have been through a ton of change. We have moved out of the house we lived in for ten years. (In the last chapter, I will go into more detail about significant recent events). We moved into a rental home to get our older boys in the school district we wanted. We moved again into a home that we built. And, we had our third son. All of these life changes happened within a matter of six months.

You know the old saying, "when you go from two kids to three kids, you go from man-to-man to zone defense?" That is exactly what we have done. For the past several months, my wife has taken the majority of the responsibility with our newborn, Lawson. I have taken most of the responsibility with our older two boys, Ethan (8) and Mason (6).

We have been so occupied with school, sports, getting settled in the new house, and the new demands of a new baby that we have taken very little time to make time for ourselves. When this happens to us, we both seem to "spin in different orbits."

Since I have started The Good Dad Project, I have had the opportunity to speak to so many Moms and Dads. So many have told me that if they could have done one thing a bit different, it's that they would have made their spouse more of a priority. Most parents will make the kids their first priority, which makes sense.

However, I would challenge that. We need to make our spouse our first priority.

If you ask most women what they desire most in their marriage, it's communication and connection.

If we don't make time to connect and nurture a healthy relationship, the rest of the family will crumble along with the marriage. Without that connection to your spouse, you could easily become two strangers who are living under the same roof. It's so easy to get so busy and caught up in the day to day activities that we forget to give attention to the one person who matters most. Once that connection is lost, it could be lost forever. We all reach points in relationships where we have a fine line. Once it is crossed and one person has emotionally/physically checked out, it's extremely difficult to get that back.

TIP #1
MAKE TIME FOR A 10 MINUTE DAILY CONNECTION

One of the things that Jess and I have done over the past year is carve out ten minutes every single day to talk. We usually take ten minutes right before bed to catch up on our day. The reason we do it right before bed is because it is virtually impossible to connect and communicate while three little boys are awake. We have attempted to connect at several other times during the day and it just doesn't work for us. I think back on the times we have tried to do it during different times of the day and it makes me laugh. Trying to catch up at the dinner table is a huge challenge. We usually can't get through three sentences without hearing "mommy...mommy....mommy...daddy...daddy...daddy." As much as we love hearing those words from the boys, it can be frustrating when we are trying to have adult conversation. So, we have reset that entire expectation. Dinner is no longer about Jess and me. In all honesty, it was completely moronic to think that it should be. Dinner should be about the whole family and centered around discussion, fun, and joking with the kids. After all, dinner is about everyone and the whole family.

So, we have made it a point to have what we call "pillow talk." (I know what you are thinking. Get your mind out of the gutter!) All kidding aside, we call it pillow talk because we are usually laying down, facing each other, tv and electronics are off, and there are no distractions. It is time that is just for us to catch up. The greatest thing about carving out these ten minutes is that it is never just ten minutes. It turns into twenty minutes, thirty minutes, and sometimes even sex! And why shouldn't it? If two people are connected on an emotional level, then the physical part is even more improved.

I have no doubt you know this already, but men express love and affection through sex. Sex and physical affection is how we men feel most loved and connected. Women, on the other hand, feel most love through communication and connection. The more you fill her need of communication and connection, the more likely the situation will turn into something that also fulfills our need of physical affection. The best part about this whole thing is we are both getting our needs completely met which makes the connection even more amazing.

TIP #2
THE NON-NEGOTIABLE MONTHLY DATE NIGHT

When was the last time you and that beautiful bride of yours went out on a date, just the two of you? If it has been within the last thirty days congrats! You are definitely the minority. When our lives are busy with the daily grind and the kids, we tend to put quality time with our spouse on the back burner. It's nothing we intend to do on purpose. We are simply too busy and it is not on the forefront of our mind. However, the monthly date night is an absolute must! The monthly date nights are essential because:

- They get us out of the daily grind

- They give us an opportunity for connection and intimacy

- They give us time to catch up and feed the relationship

- They give us an opportunity for communication without distraction

In all honesty, the hardest thing about a date night is scheduling it. If I can give you any advice it would be to schedule your date nights and your babysitters for the next three months. Literally sit down with your wife, get out the calendar, pick the dates for the next three months, and book the babysitters. Once the dates are set and the babysitters are booked, it becomes non-negotiable. There is no backing out or deciding to stay in at the last minute. Make sure you get out and enjoy yourselves. Give each other the gift of presence, connection, and communication at least once per month. I promise the payoff is huge. The dividends are paid in the form of enriched relationship, better connection, and more intimacy.

TIP #3
BE THERE

"Be there" simply means be powerfully present in the moment with your spouse. Nothing will turn a woman off faster than a man who doesn't listen. Obviously, we know that women are wired a bit differently compared to men when it comes to intimacy and the feeling of love. Most men feel loved through words of affirmation/appreciation and physical touch. However, women feel loved when they feel heard, seen, connected, and understood. As a result, love and intimacy for a woman starts with verbal and emotional connection.

So, what is the solution to ensuring you will not lose that connection? Below are some helpful hints that will help you right out of the gate.

The TAKEAWAY TIPS

1. **Find ten minutes per day to connect.** I know it sounds crazy, but try it. It can be first thing in the morning, a phone call in the afternoon, or at the end of the night.

2. **Have a date night at least once per month.** Get out of that house and go do something together without the kids. Literally schedule it and make sure the sitters are ready to go. It can be a hobby you both enjoy. It can be dinner at your favorite restaurant. It can be anything that you both enjoy and encourages you to interact with each other. However, DO NOT go see a movie. Why? Because you are not interacting. You are not connecting. The whole point of getting out for a date night is to have an interactive experience. It's really hard to do that when you go to the movies.

3. **Be there.** Be powerfully present in the moment with your spouse. Women feel love when they are seen, heard, understood, and connected.

Making time for each other is so critical. The connection with your wife is extremely important for the health of the entire family. Making small adjustments to your daily routine to make time for your wife can really make a positive impact.

CHAPTER 8
CHOOSE *Your* FRIENDS WISELY

"You are the average of the five people you spend
the majority of your time with."—Jim Rohn

Have you ever heard the above quote by Jim Rohn?

Just think about that for minute: You most likely fall right in the middle of your five closest friends. You are probably the average from body weight, to financial income, to level of education, etc.

Moreover, this phenomenon spills over into our overall attitude. Have you ever noticed that negative people attract other negative people? It is also known that people who have a very positive outlook attract others who have a very positive outlook.

For this particular chapter, I want to take you through an exercise that will encourage you to take a closer look at those you chose to surround yourself with. Most likely this group will fall into two different categories:

1. **Energy Boosters.** These are the people you feel good being around. They are positive, upbeat, and have an overall positive view of life. They smile a lot. They have very open and positive body language. They use open gestures when talking, hold eye contact during a conversation, and smile a lot. They often ask others about their lives and engage in fruitful conversation. You can literally feel their energy when you are in their presence. They are also the people who are usually the life of the party. They can completely change the atmosphere of a room when they walk in. I am not talking about people who put on a fake persona of being happy. These are people who are genuinely happy.

2. **Energy Drainers:** These are the people we don't necessarily feel the best being around. They are usually negative, down, and have a poor outlook on life. These are the folks who are always complaining about work, bills, co-workers, etc. Usually the sky is just falling down on them. They usually don't have open or positive body language. Arms can be crossed, a scowl or sour look on their face, and do not hold eye contact. They don't smile very often. Their conversations usually center around gossip and potentially tearing others down. Are you getting the picture yet?

Now, here's what I want you to do. Think of your five closest friends. Think about *education, income level, body weight, sphere of influence, ambition, and overall thirst for life.* Most likely, you fall somewhere in the average for all those categories.

Let's take it one step further: Are these five people "energy boosters" or "energy drainers?" Most likely the group will have at least one of each. Do they build you and others up or do they tear you down? Do you feel energized, invigorated, and positive when you are around them or do they take the wind out of your sails?

Once you have made the decision to be a Dad with purpose and to be the best version of yourself, it is critical to surround yourself with others who have a similar mission. It's important to surround yourself with people who support and care about you. Additionally, these types of relationships are deeper than just the typical friendship.

Most of us men have had the same friendships for several years. In fact, if you think about it, you have most likely not formed a deep friendship with someone in quite some time. That's because the older we get, we become even more guarded and make less friends. Most of us men have friendships where we talk about "safe stuff." Meaning, we talk about the same handful of things every time we meet. We talk sports, politics, the news, the weather, kids, and the simple things in life. Very, very rarely do we share something extremely deep that makes us remotely vulnerable. Even if we are struggling with something as a father, we will rarely talk about it with a friend for several reasons. We don't want to be viewed as "weak." We don't want to be viewed as "not up to the task." We don't want to be made fun of or belittled for a struggle.

Here is the big take away here: *You need those deep, supportive, and positive relationships in your life. Sometimes the friendships we have had the longest time don't serve us in this way. While these friendships are enjoyable, when push comes to shove and we need some reinforcements, they sometimes are not the best. Sometimes we need something more out of a friendship.*

You need deep, supportive, and positive relationships in your life.

About two years ago, I was invited to go on a weekend men's retreat through my church. I accepted the invitation. However, the closer I got to the beginning of the retreat, the more apprehensive I got about going. I knew no one on the retreat. I only knew that it was a retreat of all men. There was no cell phone use, no TV, no internet, and no contact with the outside world for two days. To be honest, it really freaked me out. I didn't know what to think about any of it.

With the support of Jess, I decided to go ahead and go through with it. What I found on that weekend has literally changed my life. While I was on this retreat, I was able to talk to other men (participants) who were going through very similar struggles. Struggles as a man, a father, a son, a friend, and a husband. The weekend really gave all of the participants an opportunity to be real and talk about anything that was on our minds. One of the biggest takeaways I learned from that weekend is we are not connected in our perfection—or what we want people to think is perfection. We are actually connected by our vulnerabilities, our imperfections, and our flaws. I was able to form friendships with other men and fathers with whom I would not have been able to otherwise.

> **We are not connected in our perfection—**
> **or what we want people to think is perfection.**
> **We are actually connected by our vulnerabilities,**
> **our imperfections, and our flaws.**

I am proud to say that here I am two years later with those same friendships I made on that weekend. The greatest thing about these friendships is that they run much deeper than some of the relationships I have had for several years. Once a month, there is a group of ten of us that meet. Normally, it is a very simple gathering. We get together at someone's home. One of the coolest things about the monthly meetups is that we each go around the table and give an update on our lives. We talk about the great things that have happened that month and we also talk about something that we might be struggling with. No matter the struggle, there is never any judgment from those who are listening. There is only caring, empathy, and support. Once we are done sharing what we are proud of and what we are struggling with, each of the listeners will give their supportive feedback and advice on the situation. Words cannot describe how empowering and impactful this type of group has been on our lives.

Now, I am not saying that you need to do a men's retreat or hold monthly meetups—not in the least. What I am saying, is how empowering and impactful it is to have really deep friendships. It is so critical for us as men to have this type of support. I encourage you to find this type of friendship in one person or a group. You need relationships that can help support you when you are struggling most. You need friendships that build you up and never tear you down. When life throws its best punches, it is critical to have someone in your corner.

The TAKEAWAY TIPS

1. Believe it or not, some of the friends you have had for the majority of your life might not be the best to spend the majority of your time with. I'm not saying you need to go out and cut ties with friends who you have known for ten, fifteen, or twenty years. What I am saying is you may want to limit the amount of time you spend with those folks if they are not the most supportive and positive bunch.

2. Seek out one friend (or a group) who you can go to when times get tough. We all need positive relationships in our lives.

3. You can find these relationships in churches or men's groups.

CHAPTER 9
How TO FIND HAPPINESS, PATIENCE, & PEACE OF MIND... EVEN IF IT'S THE WORST DAY OF YOUR LIFE

THE MYTH:
"I am having the worst day of my life. I am so stressed out. I will be happy if I could just have or do (fill in the blank)."

Do any of these statements sound familiar? Do you say them to someone else at least once a day? Do you say them to yourself quietly, but yet hear the voice so loudly?

If so, you are not alone.

Most of us are saying these things out loud or to someone else several times a day. The problem with this type of dialogue and thought process is it's absolutely devastating to our confidence and enjoyment of life.

I understand this thought process and self-fulfilling prophecy far too well, because I lived it for far too long.

Like so many, I focused on something external that I thought would make me happy. In my mind, I always had thoughts of:

"If I only had a higher paying job I would be less stressed and have more happiness."

"If I had less debt, I would have more money and I would be happy."

"If I had a better manager/supervisor, I would love my job and would have more opportunity for promotion."

"If I could lose weight and get in better shape, I would be happier and feel better about myself."

There are so many "if I could just," "if this was different," or "if things were this way, I would be happier" statements we make.

That type of perspective is all based on external factors. In a nutshell, it is our individual "story" of why we cannot achieve happiness and fulfillment. We base our happiness, enjoyment, and fulfillment on the story of why we cannot have our happiness, enjoyment, and fulfillment.

Make sense? I know it may sound a bit confusing, but it is really quite simple. The exact reason we are not happy and fulfilled is because of the story or inner dialogue we are saying to ourselves.

It is the trickiest and most vicious cycle in our human mentality.

Let's break down each one of those statements:

STATEMENT/STORY #1
"If I only had a higher paying job, I would be less stressed and have more happiness."

BELIEF

More money and higher paying job means happiness. Therefore, I must not be happy and must stay unhappy until I find a higher paying job.

THE VICIOUS CYCLE

You are setting yourself up for unhappiness, dissatisfaction, and overall lack of enjoyment of life until you find a higher paying job. Therefore, happiness will not be achieved until this happens.

THE TRUTH

Higher paying jobs do not produce happiness. For the most part, higher paying positions usually require more work, longer hours, and a potential decrease in work/life balance. Higher paying jobs can also come with more pressure and potentially less overall satisfaction.

THE SOLUTION

Your happiness does not depend on the amount of money you make. *Your happiness depends on your decision to be happy vs. making it depending on something external.* While money can make some aspects of life easier, it does not bring "happiness." Some of the happiest people in the world don't have a dime to their name. Some of the wealthiest people in the world struggle with life crippling depression and anxiety. The late Robin Williams is a prime example. Robin had all the money he could possibly desire; however, he struggled with depression.

STATEMENT/STORY #2

"If I only had a better manager/supervisor, I would have more opportunity for promotion."

THE BELIEF

As long as I continue to work for this manager, I will not achieve the career aspirations I would like to achieve. As a result, I will never be completely happy and fulfilled working for this person.

THE VICIOUS CYCLE

You are giving away your happiness, your power, and your self–worth to a manager you do not enjoy working for. Therefore, as long as you remain employed under this person you will achieve this self-fulfilling prophecy of never being fully appreciated at work. As a result, your perception will be your reality and your work life will be unsatisfactory.

THE TRUTH

Your self-worth, work ethic, qualifications, and drive are not controlled by anyone else but you. You choose to remain unhappy and unfulfilled by using your "unsatisfactory manager" as the story of why you will not move up in the company and ultimately not be happy. The absolute truth is you can simply change "your story"; you will change your perception and it will result in a different life.

AN EXTREME PERSONAL STORY
ABOUT HOW I HAD TO FIND MY HAPPINESS,
PATIENCE, AND PEACE OF MIND
DURING THE WORST SIX WEEKS OF MY LIFE

Let me preface this personal story with a few details before I get started.

First, as I sit here, right here and now, this life event that lasted six weeks just came to an end two days ago. Second, the past six weeks have been the most challenging time in my entire life. As I sit here and type the remainder of this chapter, this is the first time I have written about it. Even as I begin to write this part of the book, I am emotionally, physically, and spiritually challenged to express thoughts and feelings around it. It has literally taken me nearly two full months to finish this final chapter because of the emotional toll.

As I stated in the beginning of the book, I have four boys: Ethan (8), Mason (6), Lawson (1), and Gabriel who is now in heaven. It is currently December 30th, 2014 as I am writing this. About two months ago, Jessica and I found out we were pregnant with our fourth child. Yes, having a fourth can be daunting...but we were excited about another. My two oldest (Ethan and Mason) are only twenty months apart. It has been amazing seeing the two of them growing up together. They can be best friends and worst enemies, but at the end of the day, they still have each other. We had such a great time seeing Ethan and Mason being raised together, that we wanted to have a sibling for Lawson (our one-year-old). When we found out we were pregnant with our fourth we found out that Lawson and baby #4 would actually have the same age gap as Ethan and Mason (twenty months). It seemed perfect. Jessica was excited, I was excited, the boys were excited. It all seemed so right.

Six weeks ago, we received some news that completely changed our lives and turned our world upside down. A week prior to thanksgiving, Jessica went in for some routine blood work to make sure everything was normal and healthy. The results were not what we expected. I will never forget the day, it was the day before thanksgiving when we got the phone call from our physician.

With a very remorseful voice, our physician said, "I'm so sorry, I don't know how to say this…but your baby boy tested positive for Trisomy 13." At that moment, we had no idea what Trisomy 13 was or what it meant. All we knew was that it couldn't be good.

I won't get into all the scientific detail, but what I can tell you is that the outcome is not a good one. The short version of this extremely rare disorder is that in almost every case documented, it is fatal. Over 94% of all babies with Trisomy 13 do not live past one year. In fact, most do not survive a week. Trisomy 13 affects development of all major life sustaining organs.

Shock and devastation were the only words I can use to express what we felt once we were fully aware of what we were up against.

At first, we were in denial.

"This can't happen to us…we are good people. We pray, we pay our bills, we are involved with so much with our kids, we try and do everything possible we can right….so, how could this happen? The tests must be wrong. Tests can always be wrong. We cannot really be pregnant with a child who is going to die. We can't carry a child that we know will die within only a few days after birth. Our kids would never get over seeing their brother die. We would never get over seeing our son die."

At first, I was bound and determined to stay strong for Jess. She was devastated. My first reaction as a husband and father was to go into "protection mode" and help her take care of her emotions. I wanted so badly to take the pain away because I could see the pain in her eyes every day for those six long weeks. I can tell you I tried to remain strong, but it only lasted for a very short time. To be honest, extreme sadness, anger, devastation, and even anger towards God set in. For the first couple of weeks I couldn't wrap my arms around our situation and why it had to happen to us.

We were facing three ways our situation could turn out. All three potential outcomes were very grim.

POTENTIAL OUTCOME #1
TERMINATING THE PREGNANCY

I have never been a person who is pro-abortion. I believe every human life is valuable and has a purpose. However, given our situation, our physician informed us that most couples decide to terminate when given the prognosis of Trisomy 13. She didn't coach us to make the decision to terminate, she simply presented our options and informed us that the end result would most likely be the same. Whether we carried this child to full term or not, this child was most likely not going to live past seven days or most likely not even survive the trauma of the birth. So, given our circumstances, termination actually seemed like a more "humane" route to take. I know full well that there will be several pro-life folks reading this book and will be shocked by that statement. However, let me explain my case here. When you are given news like this, and it's your own child, your wife, and your other children who will be potentially traumatized, you are tempted to think differently, based on the unusually difficult circumstances. I'm not asking you to agree—just to empathize. It was just a brutal situation.

In the beginning stages of the six-week long process, termination seemed like the way to go. I couldn't imagine Jessica being pregnant for the next six months, knowing that our baby boy, Gabriel, would die in the NICU. Not only would he die, but we would witness his death. My fear was that he would feel pain before death. My boys would watch their brother die with tubes connected to him for life support. After thinking through all of those overwhelming and life altering thoughts, I actually thought termination would be more humane for my son, my wife, and my boys. Later, I came to realize this was not the best path to take and I will explain why later.

POTENTIAL OUTCOME #2
GOING FULL TERM & ALLOWING MY SON TO DIE ON HIS OWN

I have always believed that it is not up to another human being to take another human life. I have always believed that it is God or a higher power that is responsible for human life. So, going full term was an option as well. As we progressed along this six week journey, we were able to connect with another couple who was faced with the same fate as ours a few years ago. This other couple had decided to go full term with their child and not terminate their pregnancy. They decided that the life was not theirs to take and God would take their baby when it was time. That child lived for a few days and passed away in the hospital. The couple had told us that they were able to experience something profoundly positive in an otherwise terrible situation. They wanted the child to experience being born in a loving environment with a loving family even if it was only for hours, days, or weeks. While going full term seemed absolutely life altering for everyone in the family, somehow, someway, this family had managed to find goodness and beauty in the midst of heartache and pain. (We will talk about how you can do this too, later in this chapter).

Early on, I was still leaning more towards termination. However, this couple challenged me to think differently and going full term started to seem like more of an option. I never thought, though, that I could be strong enough to get Jess, my family, or myself through such an emotional, life-altering trauma. But still: It remained an option.

POTENTIAL OUTCOME #3
MISCARRIAGE

Miscarriage is a common outcome when the baby has Trisomy 13. In fact, 40% of pregnancies with confirmed cases of Trisomy 13 miscarry within the first two trimesters. Believe it or not, out of the three outcomes, our physician informed us that miscarriage is the "best of the worst." Why? The death of the child is peaceful and without pain, it is less traumatic compared to the other two outcomes, and the "decision" was not made by the parents to terminate.

ADDITIONAL TESTS
WITH THE SAME RESULTS

Within the first two weeks of us finding out what our son had and the three potential outcomes we faced, we had three additional tests done to confirm Trisomy 13 results. At first, we hoped that our original blood test was wrong. We hoped that somehow our lab results were read wrong. We were in immense denial; we couldn't believe this situation was unfolding. Unfortunately, all tests we performed confirmed the same result: Gabriel had this horrible fatal condition that would take his life within hours, days, or weeks after he was born.

THE FIRST THREE WEEKS AND TOUGH DECISIONS AHEAD

The first three weeks of this process were by far the worst thing Jessica and I had ever gone through. We felt the pressure of making a decision that neither of us wanted to make. Our friends and family all had opinions of what we should do, which actually, in some cases, made our situation even harder. Jessica and I both knew full well what we were up against, and everyone around us had an opinion.

For the first three weeks, we leaned heavily towards termination. Before you judge our decision, it's important to know how we decided on it. We knew this child would not survive, regardless if we decided to terminate or not. We couldn't bear the thought of carrying this child for the next six months knowing what the fate of this child would be. So many questions and thoughts entered our mind during this time.

Several thoughts and possible decisions enter your mind when faced with such a challenge:

"Is it more irresponsible to have this child, knowing he will go through the pain of death after birth?"

"How will Jessica and I ever get past such a traumatic event as watching our baby boy die?"

"Would our marriage survive such a thing?"

"How would I get Ethan and Mason through such a traumatic event as watching their baby brother die?"

"How would our family be forever changed after such a life altering event?"

It was literally as we went through the above questions over and over and over again for weeks that it seemed obviously logical that termination was perhaps more of a "responsible" (I use that adjective lightly) choice. The thought of abortion seemed absolutely horrible. Like I said, I have always believed the decision of life or death was not up to me. Not to mention something else: How could I live out the mission of The Good Dad Project if I knew I had made the decision to abort my child? However, I felt that as a father, the emotional protection of my family was stronger than any other consideration. I thought it was more "irresponsible" for us to carry this child to birth only for our family to be potentially torn apart by witnessing such a traumatic event. So, my wife and I made the decision to terminate and the date would be December 12th. That day was just a few short weeks after learning the news. We were informed that if we waited much longer than December 20th, the procedure would be much more invasive and dangerous for Jess.

As the week of December 12th approached, the thought of abortion became more and more difficult. To be honest, the stress of knowing the day was approaching was making me sick with stress, grief, and an overall feeling that we were doing something incredibly wrong. I then started questioning my decision to terminate and wondered if it was the best course of action. I asked myself questions like:

"What if the abortion of my son is what could tear Jessica and I apart? Perhaps the abortion could be more traumatic than actually watching my son die on God's Will and not ours?"

"What kind of message was I sending to Ethan, Mason, and Lawson if we gave up on this child?"

"Would it be a message that it is okay to give up in the face of life's challenges?"

On December 11th, the evening before we were supposed to terminate the pregnancy, I went to talk to my wife and tell her what was on my mind. I could tell this decision weighed so heavily on her mind as well. For the past three weeks, this situation consumed us. It was the first thing we thought of when we woke up in the morning, the last thing we thought about before bed, and every minute of the day in between. Every time we saw each other's face, our decision of what to do was the elephant in the room. I have never felt so powerless in my whole life.

When I went to her on that night of the 11th, with a choked up voice, I told her: "I don't know about you, but I don't think we should be doing this. Maybe we should wait and get a second opinion or get some counseling to help us make this decision." I saw a look come across her face that I hadn't seen in three weeks. It was a look of relief and peace.

She told me, "I'm so happy to hear you say that because I was thinking the same thing."

We hugged and both cried. For the first time in three weeks, we had taken our first step to making a decision that was accompanied by peace. We decided to make a counseling appointment the next week to discuss options.

THE COUNSELING APPOINTMENT
AND OUR FINAL DECISION

December 20th, 2014 is a day we will never forget. It was 2pm on a Saturday when Jessica and I sat in the office of a counselor that we knew very well through our church. He was a counselor who both of us had seen from time to time over the past twelve years. He knew us well and we saw him together about once per year. He was a great resource for when we would hit rough patches in our marriage from time to time.

We sat down with him and laid out the entire situation and all the options. We told him that we had leaned towards termination, but that we felt wrong going through with it. We also told him how we felt extremely challenged with the outcome of actually giving birth to Gabriel and seeing him die. We explained that we felt it was almost inhumane to do that to him and our boys. I could truly tell our dilemma really hit home with him. As we told our story and cried, he became choked up himself hearing about our struggle. I could tell the situation had really pulled on his heart as well. After we laid out the entire situation, he took a deep breath. What he said next I will never forget. He said this:

"I can see why you feel the way you do and why you are so torn in your decision. This is not a typical situation. Gabriel was conceived out of love and he has two parents who desperately want him. However, because his condition is fatal, you are faced with making a decision that will be the least traumatic. Let me offer what I know: If you decide to abort his life, I can tell you without a doubt, it will tear the both of you apart. Why? Neither one of you is wired to do it and it goes against all you stand for. When people ask you what happened, you will most likely come up with a story of miscarriage and it will become a situation with a great deal of darkness around it that doesn't represent either one of you. Over time, it may get the best of each of you as individuals and it may get the best of your marriage. However, if you decide to have Gabriel and put him in God's hands, you will be overwhelmed by the amount of love and support that will surround you. Meaning, your families, friends, and people closest to you will gather to your side. You will also send a very clear message to Ethan, Mason, and Lawson that in our family, we don't give up on anyone—No matter what the outcome is."

After hearing those words, the decision became unbelievably clear for what we should do. Jess and I looked at each other and we both knew without saying a word what our decision was going to be. It was the second time in over a month we felt peace and relief. We decided this decision was not ours to make. Gabriel was conceived out of love and we decided that we were going to go full term no matter what. If he only lived for minutes, hours, or days after he was born, he would be loved during his short time here.

Make no mistake: We were still terrified as to what the future held for our family, but we felt a sense of peace and confidence that we would face whatever happened head on.

DECEMBER 21ST

On December 21st, we made an appointment to see a high-risk physician who specialized in extreme cases like ours. We needed a physician who could safely deliver Gabriel and ensure Jessica was in no danger. We sat in his office and explained the situation. He listened to our case, read through our file and explained that in twenty years, he has never seen a Trisomy 13 baby live past a week. He decided to take our case and the first step was to do an ultrasound to see where he was measuring. Jess laid down on the exam table, we held hands, and watched as the doctor put the ultrasound transducer on her abdomen. He saw Gabriel and looked a bit puzzled. Jess and I looked the screen and saw Gabriel. There was one obvious difference from all other ultrasounds we had had with him:

There was no longer a heartbeat.

The doctor took measurements and he informed us that Gabriel had most likely passed away the week before or within the last couple of days. I cannot describe the feelings that came over both Jessica and I. We were sad that he had passed. We were relieved that he passed peacefully and without pain. We were somewhat happy that we knew he was in a better place. We also felt an incredible loss had just happened. It was literally a combination of all those feelings summed up in one moment. Even as I sit here and write about that moment, I am still feeling all of those emotions: Happiness, loss, relief, and sadness.

The doctor informed us to go home and get through Christmas and come back in one week to discuss options for removing Gabriel safely, as he was 18 weeks along and was too big for anything besides a scheduled procedure. We left his office and walked towards our car hand in hand. We cried together when we got to our car. We held each other and comforted each other the best we could.

DECEMBER 28TH : THE DAY I WILL NEVER FORGET

This six-week journey ended like I would have never expected. As I sit here and write about the experience of Sunday, December 28th, I still can't believe what actually happened. Words cannot describe it and this is the first time I have ever written about the events of that day.

It was Sunday, December 28th. The following day we were scheduled to go back to the specialist's office to discuss options for a safe procedure to remove Gabriel. Jessica, the boys, and I were getting ready for a family get-together. Jessica was in our bedroom getting dressed when suddenly I saw her run towards the bathroom. I didn't know what was happening at first, but I knew it wasn't good. The door was closed, but I could hear what was happening. Jess opened the bathroom door with a look of panic. She was hemorrhaging and saw blood all over the toilet. I knew she was in trouble and we needed help. This was definitely something we could not handle without medical help. My first thought was to get Ethan and Mason out of the house. I couldn't imagine them seeing their mom in trouble like that. I quickly called our neighbors in a panic and asked them to come over and get Ethan and Mason out of the house.

I told Ethan and Mason that the neighbor kids wanted to play and they were going over to their house for a bit. As soon as the kids were out of the house, Jessica screamed my name to come to the bathroom, where I found her crying and she told me that Gabriel was "halfway out" and she was severely contracting. I then called 911. The 911 operator told me to get Jessica on the bathroom floor and on her back. She remained on the line with me until the paramedics got to our house. The paramedics came through the front door to find Jessica and I on the bathroom floor. Jessica was lying flat on her back and I was sitting next to her holding her hand.

Examining Jess and the situation, the paramedics informed us that we were not going to make it to the hospital and we would have to give birth right there on our bathroom floor. I got behind Jess as she sat a bit upright so she could bear down on the contractions. Within just a few pushes, our eighteen-week-old stillborn son was born. He was no bigger than my hand. I could make out all of his features. He had fingers, toes, eyelids, you name it. Everything about him was human. Jessica, being the amazing mother she is, asked if she could hold him. I sat behind her, holding her upright while she held him peacefully in her hands. Words, emotions, and feelings cannot express what I felt at that moment. I was completely overwhelmed with emotion. To be honest, I couldn't believe what I was witnessing and I didn't know how to quite digest it. I can't sit here and tell you that it was peaceful. I can't tell you it was horribly sad. All I can honestly say at this point is that there are no words that can describe how I felt on that day at that moment. Perhaps several years from now, I might be able to put it into words or explain it, sort through all the conflicting emotions of pain and joy, heartache and hope, but for now how I felt and what I think remains a mystery.

The paramedics took us to the hospital so Jessica could be examined. Within one hour, we were discharged with a clean bill of health and instructions of things not to do for the next week. The entire day was very surreal. It was another day of sadness, peace, loss, and relief. That is the best I can describe it. It was emotionally overwhelming and confusing.

One week later, Jessica and I held an intimate funeral service for just the two of us. We wanted to say good-bye the most loving and respectful way.

WHY DO I SHARE THIS STORY WITH YOU?

I share this story with you because I would like to share what we learned that got us through that emotional six week roller coaster ride. While the whole experience was heartbreaking, on a practical level, I discovered a helpful two-step process that can help you discover happiness, patience, peace of mind and, by extension, become a better Dad.

STEP #1: CHANGE YOUR STORY AND PERSPECTIVE

What if I told you that the reason you actually cannot find happiness is because of the story you keep telling yourself over and over about why you can't have it? Just as we discussed this in a previous chapter, our story and perspective is truly our reality.

For instance, those six weeks I just shared were the hardest six weeks of my life. Knowing that we were pregnant with a child who would potentially die at birth could have easily been the demise of our marriage. I am not going to sit here and tell you for those six weeks, we didn't have our moments. We had some moments where we felt helpless, angry, and terrified. Those are the emotions that can wreak havoc on the best relationships. We could have easily taken our fear, anger, and feelings of helplessness out on each other. I won't lie: There were times we did. However, those times were minimal. We could have easily fallen into the trap of fighting and letting our emotions get the best of us. It would have been easy to do that had our "story and perspective" been one of defeat and fear.

It would have been easy to believe, *"Jessica and I are going through a really rough time in our marriage and I don't know if we are going to make it. We fight over the smallest things. We are no longer close and feel extremely distant from each other. Every time we see each other, all we can think about is the anger we feel that we are going to watch our son die. Therefore, all we do is fight. This will most likely tear us apart."*

Being completely honest with you, the above "story/perspective" that you just read could have EASILY become a very harsh reality. Do you know why? It's because the above "story/perspective" is real and reactionary. It was the perspective that my fight or flight mind wanted to buy into. Keep in mind: our brains are very primal when it comes to struggles, emotion, and feelings of defeat. Our minds want to set us up for the worst disaster to give us the feeling of certainty.

However...

If you want to live an amazing life and live a life where you can find your strength and happiness when you need it most, you must outsmart that primal brain of yours.

There were so many times, daily in fact, that I wanted to believe that "story/perspective." After all, it all made perfect sense to me. However, it was the exact opposite of what I wanted.

In order find my deepest strength in one of my darkest hours, I knew I had to rewrite my story of defeat. Not only did I have to mentally rewrite my story of defeat, but I had to say it out loud whenever I could.

Let me give you an example. Every time I heard that voice of defeat creeping in saying:

"Jessica and I are going through a really rough time in our marriage and I don't know if we are going to make it. We fight over the smallest things. We are no longer close and feel extremely distant from each other. Every time we see each other, all we can think about is the anger we feel that we are going to watch our son die. Therefore, all we do is fight. This will most likely tear us apart."

I consciously challenged myself to rewrite my perspective. I put myself on a mission to write a different story:

"Jessica and I are going through a challenging time. I don't know the reasons why right now. However, I know some way and somehow this is meant to make us stronger. In times where I feel we are drifting due to stress or uncertainty, I will give 100% of myself to her in every mental, emotional, and physical way possible. When we see each other's faces on a daily basis, we will hug a little longer and give 100% empathy and support to each other. We WILL get through this. We WILL survive this. Our marriage WILL NOT suffer. It will make us stronger."

I would ask that you read those two perspectives once again. After you get done reading each one, I want you to ask yourself which one you would rather live with on a daily basis, knowing our situation.

The first perspective is a "victim's mentality." The second perspective is a "strength mentality."

STEP #2: CHANGE YOUR STRATEGY

Jessica and I didn't just have to change our story and our perspective. On a practical level, we needed to think through how we were going to respond to our terrible situation. It presented a tremendous challenge and we needed a strategy for how we were going to survive. As you read, we spent hours and days thinking through our options and wrestling with what we needed to do.

In the same way, if your desire is to be the best Dad possible, you must have a plan of action. No one becomes great at something without hard work and a plan of action.

For instance, think of the greatest athletes in the world who have perfected their craft. Michael Jordan was not born one of the most amazing basketball players of all time. He worked countless hours shooting hoops, running drills, and perfecting his dribbling to become a hoops legend.

He had a goal to become the greatest. He had a plan and a strategy to practice and refine his craft on a daily basis. He would practice first thing in the morning, strength train in the afternoons, and execute drills in the evening. He made sure he did the right things outside of the court by eating a nutrient-dense diet and getting optimal sleep. Virtually, everything he did on a daily basis was centered upon one clear goal: To be the best.

My question for you is, "Are you executing the right strategy on a daily basis to be the best version of yourself as a Dad, a Husband, and a Man?"

Perhaps, at this point in your life, you are not doing everything right. Perhaps you are struggling in one or several areas of your life. You need to know here and now that it's ok and it doesn't matter what you have done in the past. It doesn't matter what you struggled with or the mistakes you have made. What truly matters is you have taken the first step to make a positive purposeful change. You wouldn't have picked up this book and read this far unless you were ready for something different.

So, let's stop right here and simply congratulate yourself. You are one step closer to action. Many simply don't get this far. Most of us will continue to live a life of struggle and discontent because we are too comfortable in our comfort zone. The ironic thing about "comfort zones" is that most of them are pretty uncomfortable if you really analyze them.

We don't grow if we stay in our comfort zone. We don't get any better in our comfort zone. We do not become one of the elite in our comfort zone. Just imagine if Michael Jordan would have been comfortable staying in his comfort zone. He would not be the elite athlete he is today.

The same goes for you.

It's now time to step up and get a strategy. I want you to formulate a strategy that will continue to challenge you, make you grow, and force you out of your comfort zone on a daily basis.

CONCLUSION

In this book, I've provided several tips and suggestions.

As a recap, these ten critical tips are the "essentials" for ramping up your strategy for succeeding as a Dad. I promise these will at least give you a very solid foundation and lay the groundwork for success.

Men, make a commitment:

- To make the daily conscious decision to simply be an AMAZING DAD.

- Choose to see the positives in any challenging situation. The positives are always there if you look closely.

- To connect with your spouse purposefully and intently on a daily basis without distractions

- To feed your patience by taking time for yourself each day to avoid burnout.

- To improve your physical health by eating the right foods and doing physical activity on a daily basis. Taking thirty to sixty minutes per day to do something active will make an enormous change in your life.

- To have a weekly date with your kids (just you and them). Pick a Saturday or Sunday for just a few hours to have dedicated time just for them and you.

- To once a year, take your kids on a one-on-one trip. Remember, it doesn't have to be elaborate or expensive. The destination or the cost doesn't matter nearly as much as the time together.

- To never measure yourself against perfection. You are human. You will make mistakes. Own them, apologize if need be, learn/grow, and move on.

- To quiet the voice of fear and feed the voice of strength. Listen or read to something uplifting every single day. There is a vast variety of books, podcasts, and Youtube videos that feed the much-needed positivity in our lives.

- To choose your peers/inner circle wisely. Identify the "energy boosters" and the "energy drainers." Cut ties or minimize time with those who want to hold you back from your full potential. Choose to spend more time with the relationships that build you up and don't tear you down. Get the toxic and negative people out of your life.

- To find your daily happiness by

  - Rewriting your story and changing your perspective

  - Developing a strategy/plan and putting it into practice

Well, that's it. Now, as you finish up reading this book, I want to take a moment and thank you from the bottom of my heart. Being a Dad is truly one of the most amazing privileges. I want you to know I am humbled to be able to help you—even in a small way—on your journey. If all of the chapters hit home or if even just one was helpful, I am honored. Never forget how important your job is as a father and never forget you are never alone in your journey.

I wish you the best. Never hesitate to reach out and connect with me.

Enjoy your journey to the fullest,
Larry

ABOUT *The* AUTHOR

Larry Hagner is the creator of the The Good Dad Project Show, featured as one of the top podcasts on iTunes. A graduate of Southeast Missouri State University with a background in Health, Wellness, and Nutrition, Larry went on to be the founder of The Good Dad Project, a successful organization that is dedicated to helping Dads through various resources. Larry is also a dynamic speaker who has spoken for several churches, men's groups, women's groups, and couples with outstanding reviews.

Meet Larry and receive several free resources at
www.gooddadproject.com

DO YOU WANT A SPEAKER
THAT WILL MAKE AN IMPACT?

Would you like Larry to speak at your next group or event? Simply go to GoodDadProject.com/speaking and use the contact form. Tell us about your event and we will work together to create a perfect program for your audience.

CURRENT PROGRAMS INCLUDE:

1. *The Dad's Edge*—6 Simple Ways to Achieve: Unlimited Patience, Improved Relationships, and Positive Lasting Memories

2. *The Balanced Dad*—5 Essential Strategies to Achieve Ultimate Work/ Life Balance

3. *The Mom with Purpose*—5 Effective Ways to Achieve: Unlimited Patience, Improved Connection With Your Husband, and Positive Lasting Memories

4. *The Couples Connection*—5 Simple Strategies to Achieve: Improved Communication, Enhanced Understanding of Each Other's Needs, and Positive Lasting Memories

Here is what people are saying about Larry Hagner's presentations and workshops:

"I am grateful for the Good Dad Project. The men of Assumption who gathered last fall to share stories and encourage each other to be faithful disciples and good fathers amidst so many obstacles were well rewarded. Larry brings an enthusiasm, a connection with men's lived experience and a wisdom which inspire men to stay the course. The Good Dad Project is helping the men of Assumption to live our mission and make a difference in the world."
Father Mitch Doyen, Pastor at Assumption Parish

"We had the pleasure of having Larry speak at our church over the past few months. His Dad's Edge program was very impactful to many of our fathers, and to me, personally. Larry's straightforward and authentic approach makes it very easy to adopt his strategies to being a more engaged father. He shares many of his own personal stories which allow all men to relate and appreciate Larry's passion. Personally, I enjoyed Larry's "Couples Connection" session the most as it helped reinforce the importance of my relationship with my wife in relation to being a better father. We look forward to having Larry back again soon!"
Mike Small, Men's Ministry at Morning Star Church

"Direct, powerful and intensely real, The Dad's Edge creates a new roadmap for those wanting to step more personally, emotionally and fully into their role as a dad. Challenging the dad stereotypes and unreasonable expectations, Larry Hagner offers personal perspectives and practical strategies on what it means to be a modern dad, one who shows up bigger, bolder and better to ourselves and to our kids."
Jay Forte, Author, Speaker, and Life Coach – "The Greatness Zone"

"I promise to be a good father to my children. I want them to know that they, along with my wife, are the most important parts of my life and I will always be there for them. And when I'm gone, I want them to say that I gave them 100% of me"…..
These are just a few things that I have always thought but never vocalized or had a plan to achieve. Now, with the help of the Good Dad Project, I have a proactive approach to achieve this! The GDP gives me the knowledge and tools to make this attainable as well as a forum to discuss the current struggles I am going through. Thank you, Larry, for everything you have done for me and my family.
Jason Boschert, Men's Ministry St. Cletus Church

TUNE IN TO ONE OF THE TOP FAMILY SHOWS ON ITUNES!

The Good Dad Project Show is a fun, entertaining, and enlightening look at fatherhood and parenting. Larry Hagner breaks down common challenges of fatherhood and makes them easy to overcome. Tackling the world of fatherhood can be a daunting task when we try to do it alone. The mission of The Good Dad Project Show is to help Dads become the best, strongest, and happiest version of themselves. Simple as that.

HEAR WHAT OTHERS ARE SAYING ABOUT
THE GOOD DAD PROJECT SHOW:

"I really love this podcast. So many father-themed shows are cheese-tastic, but I found this podcast to be the perfect blend of thoughtful reflection and practical tips. The content is outstanding and so helpful for any Dad in any type of situation. A must listen! —**Vaughn K.**

"If you are looking for a resource to become a better parent to your child, then look no further and listen to The Good Dad Project! All of us have challenges with parenting and up until now there has not been a lot of resources for Dads. A big thank you to Larry for all your hard work in teaching us to become better fathers. This is fantastic! I am looking forward to many future podcasts! —**Jim A.**

"It makes me so happy to see these men doing great work in the world! I want to shout from the rooftops "YES!" A show like this is long overdue. Ladies, there is plenty here for you too! It's sexy to hear two men being vulnerable. As a soon to be stepmom, there is plenty of great information for me too. —**Nikki S.**

"When learning something new or when you have the desire to open your horizons, it really helps to find people you can connect with. You came to the right place with The Good Dad Project. We all struggle. We all have insecurities. What better place to come to in knowing you are not alone while listening to Larry and Shawn tell it like it is and not holding back. The Good Dad Project tackles subject matters about family, health, children, spouses, sex, fears, doubts, joys, loss, and so much more with an open and honest heart. You don't have to be a DAD to listen. I am a mom of a thirteen-month-old boy and a very supportive husband. I find Larry's material extremely useful for my own life and growth. Take a listen, you will leave with a smiling heart and a desire for more! Thanks Good Dad! YOU ROCK! —**Noelle V.**

SUBSCRIBE FOR FREE ON iTUNES OR STITCHER RADIO

Made in the USA
Lexington, KY
30 July 2016